THE CATHOLIC UNIVERSITY OF AMERICA
CANON LAW STUDIES
No. 225

# RELIGIOUS WHO ARE KNOWN AS *CONVERSI*

## AN HISTORICAL SYNOPSIS AND COMMENTARY

BY
THOMAS AQUINAS BROCKHAUS, O.S.B., A.B., J.C.L.
MONK OF ST. BENEDICT'S ABBEY, MT. ANGEL, OREGON

A DISSERTATION
SUBMITTED TO THE FACULTY OF THE SCHOOL OF CANON LAW OF THE CATHOLIC UNIVERSITY OF AMERICA IN PARTIAL FULFILLMENT OF THE REQUIREMENTS FOR THE DEGREE OF DOCTOR OF CANON LAW

THE CATHOLIC UNIVERSITY OF AMERICA PRESS
WASHINGTON, D. C.
1946

*Imprimi Potest:*
✠ THOMAS MEIER, O.S.B.,
*Abbas Monasterii sancti Benedicti,*
*Apud Montem Angelorum in Oregon, die 4 octobris 1945.*

*Nihil Obstat:*
THOMAS J. TOBIN, V.G., S.T.D., J.C.D., LL.D.,
*Censor Deputatus,*
*Portlandiae in Oregon, die 17 decembris 1945.*

*Imprimatur:*
✠ EDUARDUS D. HOWARD, D.D.,
*Archiepiscopus Portlandensis in Oregon,*
*Ex aedibus Curiae, die 18 decembris 1945.*



MURRAY & HEISTER—WASHINGTON, D. C.
PRINTED IN THE UNITED STATES OF AMERICA

 9

## TABLE OF CONTENTS

## PART TWO

## CANONICAL COMMENTARY

# FOREWORD

The purpose of the present dissertation will be to set forth the Church's legislation for *conversi* as enacted in the Code of Canon Law. A number of Constitutions of the Roman Pontiffs, as also instructions of the Sacred Congregations, will be cited at some length, inasmuch as they furnish a guide for the interpretation of the sacred canons and for the determination of the manner in which they are to be observed. It has seemed necessary to devote a considerable portion of this study to an investigation of the origin of the *conversi* institute and to a sketch of its historical development, in order to determine as precisely as possible its position in the present-day Canon Law for religious.

The writer wishes to take this opportunity to express his sincere gratitude to his Abbot, Rt. Rev. Thomas Meier, O.S.B., for having given him the opportunity to take graduate studies in Canon Law at The Catholic University of America. He wishes to thank also the members of the Canon Law Faculty of the University for their instruction, guidance and encouragement. Finally, tribute must be paid to the memory of the writer's seminary professor in Canon Law, Rev. Charles Augustine Bachofen, O.S.B., D.D. (+ December 3, 1943), who drew up the first outline of this dissertation.

# INTRODUCTION

There are several kinds of non-clerical religious in the Roman Catholic Church, and the *conversi* are but one species of these religious. The *conversi* do not make up a universal homogeneous institute that is the same everywhere, but they are as different as the various religious orders and congregations in which they are found.[1] Further, the name *conversi*, besides being used to designate various kinds of religious, has in the past been applied to certain individuals who, although they led a quasi-religious life, were not canonically religious.

The object of this dissertation is to summarize and comment upon the special canon law for the *conversi* who are religious. Not all non-clerical religious are *conversi*, nor are they governed by the laws explained here. Only those expressly called *conversi* in the constitutions of their order or congregation, and those whose status in their communities, as will be explained in the course of this dissertation, makes them juridically *conversi*, are governed by the Church laws under consideration here.

Although the Church has promulgated a large body of law for them, she has never issued a comprehensive *system* of general legislation for the government of *conversi*. Detailed legislation for these religious has always been a matter proper to the respective orders and congregations, and when the constitutions of these various bodies have been officially approved by Rome the binding force of their statutes has not extended beyond the members of the institutes in question. Thus, for example, if the *conversi* are not to be considered "monks," it is because the constitutions say so; if they do not make solemn vows, it is again because the constitutions say so, and not because of any restriction by the general laws of the Church. The general laws the

[1] Cf. Ernest, *Our Brothers* (Indianapolis: Scott, Foresman and Company, 1931), *passim*. This work lists and briefly describes 63 lay religious brotherhoods in the United States, but does not specify which brothers are *conversi*.

Church has made regarding *conversi* have covered only certain specific aspects of their government, and have always left the constitutional status of auxiliary lay religious in their respective institutes intact.

*Conversi,* in the meaning of the term defined or described in most of the constitutions, are a second, non-clerical or non-monastic group of religious devoted *ex professo* to manual labor in clerical or monastic communities admitting this additional class.[2] This is the traditional legal situation. As a matter of fact, many *conversi* in the United States lead a more monastic life than their constitutions admit, and would perhaps benefit by having these laws brought up to date.[3] General Church legislation for *conversi* refers to them as they are actually found in their respective orders and congregations, where their status is fixed by the constitutions.

General Church law has always maintained a uniform subordination of the lay members to clerics in clerical religious institutes. It is not this divinely established hierarchy of orders, however, that determines the position of most of the lay religious known as *conversi.* For, besides this, the Church also recognizes in their case a domestic hierarchy of status within such religious organizations as have constitutions providing for a distinction of their members into various classes. This medieval juridical institute persists even today, when the *conversi* include all the non-clerical members of the majority of such organizations.

There are many examples of non-clerical religious institutes extant today, notably teaching and nursing congregations, wherein lay brothers have the full government, and labor directly at the chosen work of their communities,[4] but such brothers are not *conversi.* If these teaching brothers in turn have "lay brothers"

---

[2] Oesterle, *Praelectiones Iuris Canonici,* I (MS instar, Romae: Collegio S. Anselmi, 1931), 283. This work will be cited as *Praelectiones.*

[3] Cf. Esser, "Comment,"—*Report of the Benedictine Brother Instructors' Convention, 1942* (St. Meinrad, Indiana: The Abbey Press, 1943), p. 120.

[4] Schuetz, *The Origin of the Teaching Brotherhoods,* A Dissertation Submitted to the Faculty of Philosophy of the Catholic University of America in Partial Fulfillment of the Requirements for the Degree of Doctor of Philosophy (Washington, D. C., 1918), p. 6.

as auxiliaries to look after community needs, then these latter are sometimes *conversi*.[5]

Historically, *conversi* who were full-fledged religious and at the same time an auxiliary element in monastic communities, first appeared near the end of the eleventh century in the Benedictine abbey of Hirsau in Germany and its affiliates.[6] They were more firmly established by the Cistercians, "the first real Order,"[7] where they were introduced for the express purpose of enabling the monks to keep the Rule of St. Benedict. The Latin names for lay brothers of this kind, like *frater laicus, barbatus*,[8] *frater exterior, conversus laicus barbatus*, all have the same meaning and merely express the various characteristics by which the lay brothers were distinguished from the choir monks.[9]

In this dissertation the practice of the Code defined in canon 490 is observed:

> Whatever is enacted for religious, although the terminology include only men, applies equally to women, unless the context or the nature of the case demand otherwise.[10]

---

[5] Oesterle, *Praelectiones*, I, 283–284.

[6] Deroux, *Les Origines de l'Oblature bénédictine*, "Les Éditions de la Revue Mabillon," I (Vienne: Abbaye Saint-Martin de Ligugé, 1927), p. 95. This work will be cited as *Les Origines*.

[7] Lortz-Kaiser, *History of the Church* (Milwaukee: Bruce, 1938), p. 216.

[8] Martène *(De Antiquis Monachorum Ritibus* [Antuaerpiae-Venetiis, 1764], p. 240) quotes sources stating that the *conversi* wore beards to show they were different from the choir monks.

[9] Hoffmann, *Das Konverseninstitut des Cisterziensordens in seinem Ursprung und seiner Organization*, Freiburger historische Studien, I (Freiburg, 1905), p. 9. This work will be cited as *Das Konverseninstitut*. Deroux (*Les Origines*, pp. 1, 114) mentions a number of other names, all somewhat similar in meaning, but used at different times and places: *oblatus, donatus, devotus, commissus, frater illeteratus, hospites plenarii, prebendarii, matricularii, fratres conscripti, confessi*, etc. But these names were sometimes used in contradistinction, like the Carmelite *semifratres*, to the term *conversi*.—Lezana, *Summa Quaestionum Regularium* (Venetiis, 1654), I, 183.

[10] "Quae de religiosis statuuntur, etsi masculino vocabulo expressa, valent etiam pari iure de mulieribus, nisi ex contextu sermonis vel ex rei natura aliud constet." Translations throughout this dissertation are the writer's unless otherwise noted.

# PART ONE

# HISTORICAL SYNOPSIS

## CHAPTER I

## THE ORIGIN OF THE *CONVERSI* AS A DISTINCT CLASS OF RELIGIOUS

The monastic state has no clerical connotation, and when a priest enters a monastery the fact of his ordination makes him no more a monk than his lay confrères are monks. This is laid down in the *Rule* of St. Benedict, a document of importance to the present study, because it was in Benedictine abbeys that the institute of *conversi* was first founded. St. Benedict's *Rule* was the universal religious code in the West, except in the Celtic Church, from the eighth century[1] until the institution of regular canons in the tenth and the rise of the Mendicant Orders in the thirteenth. The introduction of *conversi* as a new class of religious by the reformatory Benedictine congregations in the eleventh century was, historically, an innovation in monasticism.[2]

In his *Rule* St. Benedict had abolished all differences, except those based on clerical orders, among the men who came to join his monastery, and commanded the abbot to make no distinction of persons in the community, "nor to let one of noble birth be put before him that was formerly a slave."[3] Regarding priests he said:

> If any one in priestly orders ask to be received into

[1] McCann, *St. Benedict* (New York: Sheed and Ward, 1937), p. 253, citing the Chapter of Aachen in 817; Knowles, *The Monastic Order in England* (Cambridge: University Press, 1941), pp. 3, 25.

[2] Cf. Heimbucher, *Die Orden und Kongregationen der katholischen Kirche* (3. ed., 2 vols., Paderborn: Schoeningh, 1933–1934), I, 204. To be cited as *Orden und Kongregationen.*

[3] C. 2—Hunter-Blair's English translation (4. ed., Fort Augustus: Abbey Press, 1934), p. 19.

> the monastery, let not consent be too quickly granted him; but if he persist in his request, let him know that he will have to observe all the discipline of the rule, and that nothing will be relaxed in his favor. . . . Let him, nevertheless, be allowed to stand next the abbot, to give the blessing, and to say Mass, if the abbot bid him do so. Otherwise, let him presume to do nothing, knowing that he is subject to the discipline of the rule; but rather let him give an example of humility to all. And if there be a question of any appointment, or other business in the monastery, let him expect the position due to him according to the time of his entrance, and not that which was yielded to him out of reverence for the priesthood. If any clerics should desire in the same way to be admitted into the monastery, let them be placed in a middle rank; but in their case also, only on condition that they promise observance of the rule, and stability therein.[4]

## §1. Distinction between "Oblati" and "Conversi"

Although there was no distinction among Benedictine monks according to their rule, they fell naturally into two groups differentiated according to the age of entrance into religion, the one made up of those who had been offered to the monastery in tender youth by their parents,[5] and the other consisting of those who came to the monastery after having lived for some time in the world.[6] The former were called *oblati,* from the Latin participle for "offered," as they were offered to the monastery by their parents; the latter came to be called *conversi,* as they were "converted" from a secular way of living to the religious life.[7]

---

[4] C. 60—Hunter-Blair, *op. cit.,* p. 161.

[5] C. 59. St. Benedict has four chapters in his *Rule* governing the manner of receiving recruits into religion: c. 58, the mode of admitting adults into the community; c. 59, infants; c. 60, priests and clerics; and c. 61, monks from other monasteries.

[6] C. 58.

[7] This conversion to the religious life was analogous to the conversion from infidelity to Christianity known from the Church's very beginnings. Cf. *Thesaurus Linguae Latinae* (Lipsiæ, 1900–), IV, 868–869, s. vv. *converto, conversus;* St. Augustine, *Speculum,* V, De conversione et contemptu saeculi—*Corpus Scriptorum Ecclesiasticorum Latinorum* (Vindobonae,

The contrast between *conversus* and *oblatus* (known sometimes also as *nutritus*) is well portrayed in the *De similitudinibus* of the English monk Eadmerus, found among the works of St. Anselm:[8]

> Since the order of monks is made up of *conversi* and *nutriti*, we would like to note here a certain rivalry between these two classes. The *nutriti* assert that they are faultless and unstained by the sordidness of the world because they have led a pure life from infancy and have spent all their labors in the service of God, whereas the exact opposite is true of these others, who are therefore an inferior kind of religious. But the *conversi* aver that they are wise to the ways of the world and it is their skill in handling the affairs of the monastery that procures the very necessaries of life for the *nutriti*; that furthermore they have a zeal for the good of the order, whereas these others do not bother themselves overmuch, and that therefore they are the better monks.

These two elements of the *ordo monachorum* were equal[9] and had to perform the same monastic duties. The *oblatus* and the *conversus* were bound alike to assist at the divine office in the oratory and to take their turns at serving at table and in the kitchen.[10]

When no hindrance to the clerical state was found in one possessed of personal merit and the proper education, the abbot

---

1866–), XII, 330—to be cited as *CSEL;* Cassian, *De institutis coenobiorum,* lib. 4, c. 1—*CSEL,* XVII, 49. It cannot be said, however, that a distinction between *conversi* and *oblati* can be derived from the text of chapters 58 and 59 of St. Benedict's *Rule* itself, as in chapter 58 "it is now an established fact that St. Benedict did not use the word *conversio* but the cognate *conversatio.*"—McCann, *St. Benedict,* p. 148.

[8] C. 78—Migne, *Patrologiae Cursus Completus, Series Latina* (221 vols., Parisiis, 1844–1864), LXX, 1322. To be cited as *MPL.*

[9] Monachum aut paterna devotio aut propria professio facit—c. 3, C. XX, q. 1. Cf. c. 1, C. XX, q. 2; c. 6, C. XX, q. 1; cc. 2, 11, 12, X, *de regularibus et transeuntibus ad religionem,* III, 31. All citations from the *Corpus Iuris Canonici* are from the Editio Lipsiensis 2. by Aemilius Friedberg (2 vols., Lipsiae, 1879–1881).

[10] St. Benedict, *Rule,* cc. 35 and 38.

chose candidates from either group for ordination.[11] Many of the *conversi* were known for the holiness of their lives, and in the tenth and eleventh centuries members of this class of monks were to be found among the leaders in the reform, as Saints Romuald (+ 1027), John Gualbert (+ 1073), Peter Damian (+ 1072) and others.

### §2. Uneducated Monks Called "Conversi"

The name *conversus* thus came in time to be the special designation for a monk who entered the monastery only after having lived for some years in the world. But at this same time when the name *conversus* was used in contrast to *oblatus,* a new and more specific meaning began to be attached to it.

> The evolution of the meaning of *conversus* corresponds to the development of the Benedictine order, especially from the time that the order entered upon the new fields of apostolic work and education. The concentration of its whole strength in these fields led naturally to a division among Benedictine monks between those who had scholastic training in preparation for the clerical state, and who could thus be used for educational work, and those who had no such education. It was not long before the former were generally known as *literati,* and the latter as *illiterati* or *idiotae.*[12]

The identification of these latter with the *conversi* arose from the fact that those who came to the monastery in later life were generally uneducated,[13] whereas the *monachi literati* were taken for the greater part from among the *pueri oblati,* who had lived in their abbeys from boyhood and whose education was famous for the painstaking care given it.[14]

---

[11] *Ibid.,* c. 62.

[12] Hoffmann, *Das Konverseninstitut,* p. 14.

[13] *Statuta Murbacensia,* 2—Albers, *Consuetudines Monasticae,* III (Montis Casini, 1907), 81.

[14] Cf. the Chapter of Aachen (816), CXLV—*Monumenta Germaniae Historica* (Hannoverae, 1826–), *Legum Sectio III, Concilia,* II, 1 (recensuit Albertus Werminghoff, Hannoverae et Lipsiae, 1906), 419–420. The *Monumenta* will be cited as *MGH.* Cf. also *Ordo Cluniacensis* per Bernardum—Herrgott, *Vetus Disciplina Monastica* (Parisiis, 1726), pp. 200

It is to be remembered that so far *conversi* were monks in the fullest sense of the word. They vowed the same observance of the Benedictine rule as the *literati.*[15] They served at Mass and at the elaborate ritual that accompanied the celebration of the divine office. Except in choir and processions,[16] they kept the rank of their seniority everywhere according to the time of their entrance into the monastery.[17] Yet these *monachi conversi* did not flourish under the circumstances and eventually disappeared. Pope Clement V in the Council of Vienne in 1311 ordered that all *monachi* commanded to do so by their abbots should receive sacred Orders.[18]

## §3. Lay Retainers Called "Conversi"

The wealth and material prosperity that the feudal system brought to abbeys destroyed the original humble ideal of self-contained communities whose members took care of their bodily needs by working together in cooperation. The heavy farm work was then done by serfs and the monastic housekeeping, by way of abuse, was taken care of by hired servants. Thus Schroll:[19]

---

sq., "Et ut tandem de ipsis pueris concludam, difficile mihi videtur, ut ullus regis filius maiori diligentia nutriatur in palatio, quam puer quilibet parvulus in Cluniaco." A classical example of the heights of sanctity and lore to which such an *oblatus* could rise is the great Church doctor, the Venerable Bede.

[15] No essential difference arose from the circumstance that they had someone else write their profession formula for them, which they signed with a cross. Cf. St. Benedict, *Rule,* c. 58; Guidonis *Disciplina Farfensis,* lib. 2, c. 2—Herrgott, *op. cit.,* p. 88; *Ordo Cluniacensis* per Bernardum, pars 1, c. 20—Herrgott, *op. cit.,* p. 180; S. Wilhelmi *Constitutiones Hirsaugienses,* lib. 1, c. 74—Herrgott, *op. cit.,* p. 443.

[16] *Consuetudines Fructuarienses,* lib. I, cc. 5, 16, 33, 46, 48, 49, 59, 77, 78; lib. II, cc. 2, 3, 12, 15—Albers, *Consuetudines Monasticae,* IV (Montis Casini, 1911), 14, 21, 32, 51, 53, 54, 55, 58, 65, 78, 92, 102, 129, 135, 162, 163, 167, 168, 169, 185; *Veteres Consuetudines Monasterii Sancti Benedicti Floriacensis,* cc. 1, 2—*op. cit.,* V (Montis Casini, 1912), 138, 148, 149.

[17] *Ordo Cluniacensis* per Bernardum, pars 1, c. 74—Herrgott, *op. cit.,* p. 274.

[18] C. 1, *de statu monachorum vel canonicorum regularium,* III, 10, in Clem.

[19] *Benedictine Monasticism as Reflected in the Warnefrid-Hildemar Commentaries on the Rule,* Studies in History, Economics and Public Law Edited

> As reflected in the commentaries (of the eighth and ninth centuries), all the monks of the community, excepting the officials, were of equal status. There are no indications of the later medieval distinction of lay brother and choir monk. . . . That our commentaries and contemporary accounts evidence the employment of lay persons in certain departments of the monastery as well as on its tributary lands during the Carolingian period was noted in the closing pages of the second chapter.
>
> (*From chapter 2 of the work here cited:* The foregoing allusions to *servi* seem to indicate that lay help was employed in the care of the guests and the poor, in the garden and in the other outside work, but that in the monastery proper, the monks performed the services. It is specified clearly that a monk and not a layman is to serve as infirmarian. It is likewise clear that the monks performed their own laundry, cleaning, and kitchen service.)
>
> Our somewhat lengthy *excursus* on the *servitores* was introduced to establish the point that laymen were not employed in the domestic service of the monastery proper. From the economic point of view it would make little difference whether laymen were employed in the garden or in the kitchen; from the monastic point of view, however, it would not be the same. The reason is to be found in Warnefrid's explanation as to why laymen may not fill the office of infirmarian. He asks, as already noted, how a lay person who is not a member of the monastery can serve a monk any more than an eye or a foot can serve the body if not of it. Only members of the family may participate in its internal affairs.[20]

Hired servants however came to cause more and more disturbance in monasteries,[21] so the superiors began to make rules for

---

by the Faculty of Political Science of Columbia University, n. 478 (New York: Columbia University Press, 1941), pp. 52, 138.

[20] Pauli Warnefridi diaconi Casinensis *in sanctam regulam commentarium* (Monte Cassino, 1880), p. 340; Mittermüller, *Expositio Regulae ab Hildemaro tradita* (Regensburg, 1880), p. 407. These two references are Schroll's.

[21] Cf. Peter the Venerable, *Statuta Congregationis Cluniacensis,* n. 23: "It has been prescribed that no clerics or lay people be allowed to enter

them analogous to those governing the life of the religious. The beginnings of the institute, which we hear of first at Einsiedeln in Switzerland and then in Italy with the Vallombrosians, seem to have about the same characteristics: lay state, a pious life, and a loose connection with some monastery—giving their services in exchange for the patronage and spiritual direction of the monks.

If we accept Ringholz's date of the turn of the eleventh century for the *Einsiedeln Customs,*[22] this document is the first historical witness to the existence of *conversi laici,*[23] i.e., of *conversi* who were not monks but lay retainers, somewhat similar to the " religious oblates " who are not canonically religious in our own day.[24] The *Einsiedeln Customs* mention these *conversi laici* twice in their fourth chapter, the second time in connection with *barbati,* and both times prescribing that they serve as acolytes along with those members of the monastery whose voices were not of much help to the choir.[25] The fact that these retainers did practically the same work as the *monachi conversi* in contemporary abbeys suggests itself as the reason for their being called *conversi,* with the modification *laici.*

A little later the Vallombrosians used the name *conversi* for the laymen who worked as servants in the monastery.[26] In the biography of their founder, a life of St. John Gualbert which

---

the cloister or other monastic dwellings. . . . The cause of this prescription was that the goings and comings of clergy, laity, and especially lay servants, were so frequent in the cloister that it seemed to be turned into a public highway."—*MPL,* CLXXXIX, 1032.

[22] Ringholz, *Geschichte des fürstlichen Benediktinerstiftes U. L. F. von Einsiedeln,* u.s.w., I (Einsiedeln, 1904), 670–671.

[23] In contrast to *conversi monachi.*

[24] For example, *Declarationes in Sacram Regulam et Constitutiones Congregationis Helveto-Americanae O.S.B.* (St. Meinrad, Indiana: The Abbey Press, 1925), n. 91.

[25] Ringholz, *op. cit.,* p. 674. The same text may be found in Albers, *Consuetudines Monasticae,* V, 80–81; and the same prescription in the *Consuetudines Monasteriorum Germaniae,* c. 43—*op. cit.,* V, 49.

[26] For a more complete treatment of this topic cf. Mulhern, *The Early Dominican Laybrother* (Washington, D. C.:[Dominican College], 1944), pp. 8–11.

dates from the end of the eleventh century,[27] there is the following text:

> From the time that monks began to gather around him (St. John Gualbert), God, who sees into a pure heart and for whose love John sought to guide his monks according to the ordinances of the rule, sent him faithful laymen who were not monks, but whose spotless life under his direction made them almost like the religious. . . . These reliable *conversi* John without any misgivings sent to market and to take care of all outside business.

Here "faithful laymen" are called *conversi* not because they came to the monastery in later life, but to distinguish them from the monks. They were "almost like the religious" and their whole work was to take care of the house and its temporal needs.

The Vallombrosians, whose purpose was to return to what they considered the literal observance of the Benedictine rule, had no distinction between *literati* and *illiterati,* and therefore no *conversi* in the Cluniac sense, but classified all who vowed observance of the Benedictine rule as *monachi;* and thus there was no confusion of names when their lay servants were called *conversi.* There was no connection between the Vallombrosian *conversi* and those of Cluny, and it cannot be stated that the Vallombrosian *conversi* were truly religious lay brothers in the technical sense developed later.

Monastic lay servants who were not serfs[28] antedated the Vallombrosians, and some of the free servants employed in domestic duties about the monasteries lived according to a quasi-religious

---

[27] B. Andreae abbatis Sturmensis *Vita S. J. Gualberti—Acta Sanctorum* edita cura Ioannis Bollandi et Bollandianorum (Parisiis-Bruxellis, 1863–), Iulii, III, 332 sq.; and, for date, *Ibid., Commentarium praevium,* n. 23—*Acta SS,* Iulii, III, 301.

[28] Serfs had been kept for centuries before this time; they tilled the soil and were employed about the monastery as artisans, etc. Cf. Hoffmann, *Das Konverseninstitut,* p. 17, footnote, citing Guérard, *Polyptique de l'Abbé Irmion ou Dénombrement des Manses, des Serfs et des Revenus de l'Abbaye de St.-Germain-des-Prés sous le Règne de Charlemagne* (Paris, 1844), II, 307; Uhlhorn, *Der Einfluss der wirtschaftlichen Verhältnisse auf die Entwickelung des Mönchtums im Mittelalter*—Brieger-Bess, *Zeitschrift für Kirchengeschichte* (Gotha, 1877–), XIV (1894), 368.

rule, as St. Peter Damian notes in the *Instituta Congregationis Avellanensis:* [29]

> So that rule and order be kept in the house of God, and every member do his own work, the servants (*famuli*) who attend here must not depart from the regulations laid down for them, etc.

These *famuli* made a promise according to a formula analogous to the profession of the monks: " I, brother N., promise obedience and perseverance all the days of my life in this monastery, erected to the honor of God and of the holy Cross, in the fear of Our Lord Jesus Christ and for the salvation of my soul. And if I ever at any time leave here or try to run away, it shall be lawful for the servants of God who shall be here, to pursue me with full authority and bring me back to their service, even using force and violence." [30] The reason the lay servants of the monks at Fonte Avellana were not called *conversi* at the time the Vallombrosians used this name for them, was that St. Peter Damian was accustomed to apply this name to a class of monks in the Cluniac sense, and it would have been confusing had he referred it also to the servants.

The Camaldolese too had these lay servants at an early date, for, according to the *Constitutiones* of Blessed Rudolph I, fourth prior of Camaldoli,[31] St. Romuald himself when he founded that monastery placed an inn at the foot of the mountain on which it stood, where, in order to keep the monks free from all distractions, one monk and three *conversi* were assigned to take care of guests and the temporal affairs of the monastery. That these *conversi* were lay servants is evident from the fact that this is the only place they are called *conversi*, their designation elsewhere being " laymen " or " servants."

[29] C. 7—*MPL,* CXLV, 342.

[30] *Loc. cit.*

[31] Mittarelli-Costadoni, *Annales Camaldulenses Ordinis sancti Benedicti* (9 vols., Venetiis, 1755–1772), III, 512 sq. There are two constitutions, the first dated 1080; the second, which is shorter, 1085. They are the first written records of the Camaldolese customs, as St. Romuald did not set down his rules in writing.

The Benedictine monasteries of France and Germany also had lay servants. Cluny had a great number of lay folk who did not belong to the monastery proper as her *conversi* monks did, namely the *famuli,* who were servants of the religious and did the housework. Every monastery official had a definite number of these servants assigned to help him, and they had a certain hierarchy among themselves, there being *famuli mediocres* and *famuli magistri.* These servants did not take religious vows, though there were attempts to make religious of them, especially when they were to be entrusted with the more important business of the monastery.[32] There were many who did not live in the monastery at all, as is witnessed by the complaint of Peter the Venerable (+·1156) in 1146, that these household servants spoke too freely of the internal affairs of the monastery to their wives and children at home. Peter sought to replace these servants with religious at a time when lay brothers were already well organized and flourishing in the Cistercian order.[33]

## §4. The Incorporation of "Conversi Laici" into the Religious State

The embryonic foundation of the *conversi* institute as it is known today is to be credited to two zealous promoters of the Benedictine reform, who as boys had attended together the abbey school of St. Emmeram in Ratisbon. St. Ulrich of Zell (1029–1093) and Blessed William of Hisau[34] remained kindred spirits despite the great distances that separated them during their active lives, and when William's interest in Cluny brought them together again in mature age[35] they collaborated in producing two immortal works of monastic usages, the *Consuetudines Cluniacenses* and the *Consuetudines Hirsaugienses.* St. Ulrich

[32] Guidonis *Disciplina Farfensis,* lib. 2, cc. 1, 44, 45, 46, 48, 52, 53—Herrgott, *Vetus Disciplina Monastica,* pp. 88, 114 sq.; *Ordo Cluniacensis* per Bernardum, pars 1, cc. 2, 5, 6, 7, 8, 9—Herrgott, *op. cit.,* pp. 138 sq.

[33] *Statuta Congregationis Cluniacensis—MPL,* CLXXXIX, 1032–1034.

[34] Died in 1091, according to Bernoldi *Chronicon—MGH, Scriptores,* V (Edidit Georgius Henricus Pertz, Hannoverae, 1844), 451. The *Scriptores* will be abbreviated *SS.*

[35] Deroux, *Les Origines,* p. 98.

had spent his life in promoting and spreading the Cluniac reform, and Blessed William, upon being elected abbot of Hirsau, introduced the monastic *consuetudines* he had learned as a boy at St. Emmeram.[36] He did not compose the *Consuetudines Hirsaugienses,* however, until after St. Ulrich's visit to Hirsau, and it was to facilitate this work that the latter, upon request, set down the *Consuetudines Cluniacenses* in three books.[37]

In the dedicatory letter to Blessed William, with which he prefaced his collection of the *Consuetudines Cluniacenses,* St. Ulrich criticized the Swiss-German treatment of the *conversi laici.* "You are exiling this poor class, which formerly did not exist," he wrote, "too far from your monastery . . . I would like to see these lay brothers live inside the cloister and wear the same kind of habit we do. Even if they are not able to act as readers or chanters like the *literati,* they are green branches of a living tree, and if they continue to work for the *literati* as they have in the past they will attain the same reward as those they serve . . ." [38]

Abbot William acted on this suggestion with energy, as the abundant provisions and regulations he set down for the *conversi* in the *Consuetudines Hirsaugienses* prove.[39] The new *conversi* institute, brought into the monastery from outside and raised to the religious state, here meets the old, which belonged strictly to the monastic order, for Blessed William's regulations for Hirsau's *conversi* are substantially the same as those of Cluny for the *monachi conversi.*[40] He admitted them to choir, except when there were so many *literati* present as to leave no room for them:

---

[36] Herrgott, *Vetus Disciplina Monastica,* p. 375.

[37] Fischer, *Studien zur Entstehung der Hirsauer Konstitutionen* (Tübingen, 1910), pp. 19 sq. Cf. the *Codex Hirsaugiensis—MGH, SS,* XIV (Edidit Societas aperiendis fontibus rerum Germanicarum medii aevi, Hannoverae, 1883), 254 sq.

[38] D'Achery, *Spicilegium,* I, 641—*MPL,* CXLIX, 637; Heimbucher, *Orden und Kongregationen,* I, 204–205.

[39] There are more than 20 references to *conversi* in this work, most of them original, only a few being copied from the *Consuetudines Cluniacenses.* Cf. Deroux, *Les Origines,* p. 95.

[40] Deroux, *op. cit.,* pp. 100, 121.

> . . . if it should happen that some of the *conversi* should not be able to enter the choir because of the large number present, they shall wait outside and watch carefully if any one should leave. . . . Then one of them should go in and take the place left vacant.[41]

There is a special chapter entitled, "No *Conversus* Is to Absent Himself from a Sermon," and its text states the reason for this prescription: the sermon "is given especially for their benefit." [42] They do not have to know how to read:

> If it is a day when speaking is permitted in the cloister, they shall not immediately start talking when they leave the chapter. Those who can read are to take a book and sit down. But the *conversi* who do not know how to read are not required to take books. . . .[43]

Detailed prescriptions are laid down as to how the *conversi* are to serve at Mass and divine office,[44] and as to what their functions are at the community *Mandatum*.[45]

A most valuable chapter is that, "On the Promotion of the Brethren." [46] It reads in part:

> According to the *Rule* of St. Benedict (c. 63) it belongs to the abbot to promote the brethren in rank, which promotion is as follows. If for some reasonable cause he should have promoted a *conversus*, the one so promoted shall keep this rank everywhere except in church, where he is not to stand among the *literati*. For the abbot is to grant none of the *conversi* a place among the *literati*, unless one should be both of upright life and of mature age, and should have learned the chant, so that he knows how to sing and read the psalms, hymns, responsories and lessons correctly. If such a one is found the abbot shall permit him to stand in the same rank in choir that he has in the chapter and refectory. . . .

[41] Lib. I, c. 33—*MPL*, CL, 966.
[42] Lib. I, c. 49—*MPL*, CL, 979.
[43] Lib. I, c. 59—*MPL*, CL, 988.
[44] Lib. I, cc. 82, 84, 86, 92, 94—*MPL*, CL, 1008, 1012, 1015, 1025, 1026.
[45] Lib. I, cc. 100, 103—*MPL*, CL, 1035, 1038.
[46] Lib. II, c. 11—*MPL*, CL, 1049.

There are many other regulations in which Abbot William excludes the *conversi* from the place of the *literati* in choir simply because they would occasion more hindrance than help in the chanting of the divine office.[47]

Blessed William did not state that he meant to establish the *conversi* as religious distinct from the monks. The new institute evolved rather by a natural process of growth, and made no sudden appearance as a pre-conceived innovation in the monastic order. This can be inferred from his biographer Haymo:

> . . . This amiable father . . . first provided that the monks should make use of the faithful help of lay *conversi* in exterior business, and in return these brothers should receive their spiritual care from the monks, and they should imitate their religious life and discipline, as far as they are able, outside the cloister. . . . They all gather in the church for the night office, but finish their Matins sooner because of the long hours of work that await them during the day. Then those who so desire return to bed, while the rest stay on in church until the monks have finished their office. At daybreak they hear Mass. Then they go to the Chapter of Faults, where they ask forgiveness for their failings, and receive an appropriate penance from the superior. After this, those who feel it necessary go to confession, and then each takes up his day's work. . . . They have no private property, but, according to the Acts of the Apostles, "distribution was made to each, according as any one had need." [48] In transacting business they avoid not only disputes and quarrels but also idle talk. They are subject to their superiors, without whose permission they do not make any long journey. They communicate every Sunday, half of them reverently receiving the Body and Blood of the Lord one Sunday, and the other half the next; but on the great feastdays they all receive together. . . . They take turns week by week serving in the kitchen and preparing food for themselves as well as for the monks and the guests. They eat together, and serve one another. Only those who are free to do so come to the church for the day hours. As at the night office, all, or nearly all, are present for Compline. Afterwards

[47] Cf. lib. II, c. 22—*MPL,* CL, 1070.

[48] *Acts,* IV, 35.

> they go to bed in silence. Abbot William erected a suitable building at Hirsau for those who followed this manner of spiritual life, namely the new monastery in honor of the blessed Apostles Peter and Paul, and of St. Aurelius, Confessor. This was built on the south side by the labor of the members of the community, being finished in nine years and dedicated in the tenth. When the church was about to be dedicated he filled it with poor folk, who lined the walls from the front to the doors. Then the doors were closed and he ministered to them personally. . . .[49]

In the *Observationes Praeviae,* which introduce the *Vita Beati Wilhelmi* in Migne, it is stated:[50]

> Besides these hundred and fifty monks, who . . . lived under the rule of Blessed William in the monastery at Hirsau, there were other brothers, called *barbati* or *conversi,* who, giving themselves to manual labor, procured the necessaries of life for the support of the monks devoted to contemplation. "Among these," says Trithemius, "were most expert craftsmen in all the mechanical arts, who with the greatest diligence brought to completion all the buildings of the whole monastery, . . . who executed the whole ensemble of monastery and church buildings with artistic taste (as can be seen today in the sculpture of the towers). The tailors also and the tanners, the shoemakers and all the other craftsmen on whom the cloistered monks depended, are said to have been neither seculars, nor hirelings, nor other employees, but all *conversi* or bearded monks. The holy abbot William first instituted this order of *conversi* in Germany, with the help of whose labors he founded so many monasteries and provided well all that was necessary for the monks. The man of God gave them statutes based on the Holy Rule . . ."

Trithemius here cited the laws for *conversi* as recorded by Haymo and as quoted above.[51] The *Observationes* continue:

[49] *Vita Willihelmi Abbatis Hirsaugiensis* auctore Heymone, n. 23—*MGH, SS,* XII (Edidit Georgius Henricus Pertz, Hannoverae, 1856), 219–220. This passage is summarized by Mabillon and cited with approval.—*Annales Ordinis S. Benedicti* (ed. 1. Italica, 5 vols., Lucae, 1739–1740), V, 185.

[50] N. 5—*MPL,* CL, 892–893. A rubric in col. 889 states that this is reprinted from Mabillon, *Acta SS. O.S.B., saec. VI,* p. II, p. 717.

[51] Pp. 13–14.

> Distinct from the *conversi* were the *oblati,* which the same holy abbot introduced in his monastery, after the example of Cluny . . . He provided that these should not change their manner of dress, but should wear secular clothing. All business outside the monastery was assigned to them. They had a monk as their superior and director. They were given a refectory separate from that of the monks and *conversi,* lest they should disturb them.

The historical evidence indicates that Blessed William regarded his *conversi* as a class of monks distinct from those who were lettered or besides were clerics. Their inability to read or write was a circumstance recognized and accepted by the laws he made for them, providing for a separate choir or a special place in choir, for doctrinal instruction and moral exhortation, for serving instead of singing at divine services, and for promotion in rank except in choir. Abbot William's practical prescriptions governing the spiritual discipline and monastic activity of the *conversi* laid the foundation for all subsequent legislation, as it is found in the present Code of Canon Law.[52] But he had only to deal with the institute in its first fervor. It remained for subsequent legislators to define more precisely the constitutional status of the *conversi,* to insure their stability by putting a legal ban on their promotion to orders and on their transfer to another class, and, finally, to add to the time of probation and preparation for this difficult vocation.[53]

The difference between Abbot William's *conversi* and those in other monasteries of his time was that his was an institute brought in from the outside, raised from the lay to the religious state. His further institution of extern oblates shows his desire of insuring the monastic character of his *conversi.* Most important of all, Blessed William legislated merely for the *conversi laici* already on the scene. He did not of set purpose introduce lay brothers as auxiliaries to enable the monks to live a more authentic monastic life. This practical feature was added by the medieval religious orders, as will be seen in the following chapter.

[52] Cans. 509, §2, 2°; 565, §2; 610, §3.

[53] Cf. cans. 539, §1; 558; 564, §2.

## CHAPTER II

## LAY BROTHERS IN THE CISTERCIAN AND LATER ORDERS

Since it was with the Cistercians, a religious congregation of reform among the French Benedictines which became the Church's first centralized religious order, that the lay brother institute received papal approval and grew to its greatest development, a study of the Cistercian *conversi* is necessary for a complete and clear picture of these religious and their place in the history of the eight following centuries.[1] An added reason for studying the Cistercian statutes is the radical and profound influence the white monks wielded in the religious and social life of western Christendom.[2] Their legislation for their lay brothers affected the whole subsequent history of the institute.[3]

The founders of Citeaux had but a single purpose, the restoration of the literal observance of the rule of St. Benedict. When they introduced lay brothers into their monasteries they did this as part of their reformative program, with the one purpose of enabling the Cistercian monks to keep their rule perfectly. These founders were the first to put a legal ban on the aspiring of *conversi* to become monks who could be admitted to the clerical state, so that "the *conversi* occupied a place in the order of Citeaux which they had never held in Benedictine monasteries." [4]

### §1. The Aims of the Cistercian Reform

The little band of Benedictines, with St. Robert (1027–1111)

[1] Cf. Hoffmann, *Das Konverseninstitut,* for a complete treatment of the material summarized in this chapter.

[2] Cf. Knowles, *The Monastic Order in England,* p. 208.

[3] Cf. Wolter, *Praecipua Ordinis monastici Elementa* (Brugis, 1880), pp. 513–518. To be cited as *Praecipua Elementa.*

[4] Berlière, *L'Ordre monastique dès Origines au XII. Siècle* (4. ed., Maredsous: Lille-Desclée, 1927), p. 290.

at their head, who were entirely dissatisfied with the traditional monasticism under which they had taken their vows, had made one previous attempt at a reform in Benedictinism, the foundation of the abbey of Molesme.[5] Molesme however slipped into the old traditions as it grew in size and possessions, so that its founders deemed it a failure and proceeded to the establishment of a new abbey, Citeaux, which was to be armed with such safeguards as would enable it to achieve its purpose.

The Cistercians, who were bitterly critical of the traditional Benedictine observance as compared with their own,[6] saw the decline of monasticism as the result of two causes: the lack of organization with a supreme authority to enforce uniform observance of the rule to the exclusion of local contrary customs, and the feudal status and activity of the monasteries together with their continual implication in secular business. The first defect they sought to heal by founding the first real religious order, with many monasteries under one centralized government, in the Church's history. The second danger to Benedictinism, feudalism, they fought by abolishing all letting of monastery property to tenants, a program of which the lay brother institute was an essential part.

When they submitted their *Consuetudines* and *Charta caritatis* with their explanatory letter, the *Exordium parvum*, to Pope Callistus II for approval, the Pontiff gave his sanction on December 23, 1119, to the explanatory letter, which furnished a concise and complete history of the foundation of Citeaux, as well as to the *Charta caritatis* and the *Consuetudines.*[7] Chapter 15 of the *Exordium parvum* thus approved recounts the constitution

[5] Cf. *Vita S. Roberti* auctore monacho Molismensi sub Adone Abbate saeculo XIII—*Acta SS,* Aprilis, III, 676 sq.

[6] Cf. Peter the Venerable, *Epistolae,* lib. I, ep. 28—*MPL,* CLXXXIX, 112 sq.; St. Bernard, *Apologia ad Guillelmum—MPL,* CLXXXII, 895.

[7] Guignard, *Les monuments primitifs de la Règle cistercienne publiés d'après les manuscrits de l'Abbaye de Citeaux,* Analecta Divionensia, X (Dijon, 1878), Preface, p. xxvii. To be cited as *Les monuments.* Jaffé, *Regesta Pontificum Romanorum ab condita Ecclesia ad annum post Christum natum MCXCVIII* (2. ed. cura G. Wattenbach, S. Loewenfeld, F. Kaltenbrunner, P. Ewald, 2 vols. in 1, Lipsiae, 1885–1888), n. 6795. To be cited as *Regesta.*

and prescriptions for the Cistercian lay brothers who had been introduced into the order early in 1101, eighteen years before. Their institution in 1101 followed upon the decision of Abbot Alberich and his monks in a chapter held after the reception of the bull of Pope Pascal II, dated October 19, 1100, which guaranteed apostolic protection to the *novum monasterium.*[8]

After stating that the purpose of the founders of Citeaux was the full observance of the rule of St. Benedict, to the exclusion of everything to the contrary, chapter 15 of the *Exordium parvum* enumerates the abuses feudalism had occasioned in monastic life and practice:

> . . . Since they [the founders] read neither in the rule nor in the life of St. Benedict that he possessed churches or altars or oblations or cemeteries, or tithes of other men, or bakehouses or mills or farms or serfs, or that he allowed women to enter his monastery, except his sister who was buried there . . . since among the monks who were great landlords they found none who lived by their own labor and that of their oxen, they considered all this an unjust usurpation. . . .[9]

The abuses referred to had resulted from the monasteries' imitation of the secular feudal lords, whose extensive lands were worked by tenants under the supervision of *villici.*

The monasteries' *villici,* at first chosen by the abbot from among the tenants, took care of the abbeys' vast business. They grew very powerful and independent, becoming local magistrates,[10] and by their abuse of authority often antagonized the tenants besides compromising the position of the monasteries.[11] The *villici* proved so troublesome that the monasteries substituted monks in their places, and these monks soon had to take up

[8] Guignard, *Les monuments,* pp. 67, 91; Jaffé, *Regesta,* n. 5842.

[9] Guignard, *op. cit.,* pp. 61–75.

[10] Schröder-Künssberg, *Lehrbuch der deutschen Rechtsgeschichte* (7. ed., Berlin-Leipzig: Verlag Walter de Gruyter and Co., 1932), pp. 189, 212, 463, 613, 654.

[11] A *villicus* of the monastery of St. Trond in the diocese of Liége put a wall and moat around his castle to defend himself against the hirelings of the abbot.—*Gestorum Abbatum Trudonensium Continuatio Secunda,* lib. 2—*MGH, SS,* X (Edidit Georgius Henricus Pertz, Hannoverae, 1852), 343.

their residence in the farmhouses at a distance from their monasteries in order to supervise the tenants in each locality satisfactorily. Although the relations with their monasteries on the part of these monks who took the place of the *villici* were minutely regulated,[12] practical exigencies were an obstacle to the centralized organization the Cistercians deemed essential for maintaining monastic discipline. St. Benedict had written:

> The monastery ought to be so constituted that all things necessary, such as water, a mill and a garden, and the various crafts may be contained within it; so that there may be no need for the monks to go abroad, for this is by no means expedient for their souls.[13]

The monks' employment as supervisors of great feudal estates also led them to despise humble personal labor. In chapter 48 of his *Rule* St. Benedict had said:

> Idleness is an enemy to the soul; and hence at certain seasons the brethren ought to occupy themselves in the labor of their hands, and at others in holy reading.[14]

But traditional monasticism looked upon manual labor as beneath the dignity of a monk, and retained it merely as a religious ceremony in a perfunctory observance of the rule.[15] Thus Odericus Vitalis:

> The custom in Gaul is that farming should be done by farmhands and the heavier labor by serfs, but monks, who of their own free will have renounced the world to fight for the King of kings, are to sit quietly in their monasteries like the daughters of the King, seeking in their reading to discover the hidden things of the law of God and meditating without ceasing thereon in their beloved silence . . . and also doing a certain amount of

[12] *Ordo Cluniacensis* per Bernardum, pars 1, cc. 2, 5, 6, 7, 8—Herrgott, *Vetus Disciplina Monastica*, pp. 138, 139 (where these monks are called *decani*), 145, 147, 150, 151.

[13] *Rule*, c. 66—Hunter-Blair's English translation, p. 181.

[14] Hunter-Blair, *op. cit.*, p. 129.

[15] Cf. Guidonis *Disciplina Farfensis*, c. XLV—Herrgott, *Vetus Disciplina Monastica*, p. 85.

such respectable work each day as common sense and the command of their superiors dictate.[16]

## §2. The Institution of Lay Brothers as Part of the Reform

The founders of Citeaux included real manual labor even for the *monachi literati* as a part of their program of reform, but the demands on the material resources of their houses threatened to keep the monks too long at these tasks, to the neglect of the prayer and contemplation still more essential to Benedictinism.

> When these soldiers of Christ . . . looked about them to see how or by what means they could support themselves and the guests . . . who the Rule commanded were to be received as Christ Himself, . . . they decided to take lay *conversi barbati* with the permission of their bishop, and to treat them in life and in death like themselves in everything, except that they should not become monks. For it was only by taking this step, and hiring more help besides, that they could assure the monks of being able to live according to the Rule, day and night. These *conversi,* cut off from human intercourse, were to cultivate the fields and vineyards, to cut down trees and build mills, . . . to fish and take care of the domestic animals. . . . And when farms were cleared the *conversi,* and not the monks, were to take care of them, since the latter were to stay at home in their monasteries.[17]

Thus the *conversi* were introduced at Citeaux to enable the monks to lead a more truly Benedictine life. Their immediate economic purpose was subordinate to their ultimate ascetic one, and it was their labor that enabled the monks to lead a balanced Benedictine life, without the undue solicitude for material necessities the economic system was forcing upon them. "These *conversi* whom we need as helpers we receive into our care as we do monks, and we consider them as much our brethren and partakers in our spiritual and temporal goods as the monks." [18]

---

[16] *Historia ecclesiastica,* pars 3, lib. 8, n. 25—*MPL,* CLXXXVIII, 639.

[17] *Exordium parvum,* c. 15—Guignard, *Les monuments,* p. 77.

[18] *Inst. Cap. Gen. collecta anno 1134,* c. 8—Guignard, *op. cit.,* p. 251.

"The first fathers of Citeaux abolished of set purpose both the oblation of infants and the education of boys within the monastery. . . . An early statute, giving precision to the *Consuetudines,* decreed that no novice was to be received under the age of fifteen, and no boy taught in the monastery, unless he were already at least a novice. . . . The division of the choir-monks into *nutriti* and *conversi* thus vanished; all Cistercians were in the old sense of the term *conversi,* but the name was transferred by them to the new class of laboring monks which they introduced into northern lands and came to bear the meaning which it has ever since retained." [19]

The first written synthetic and detailed rule for lay brothers dates from the first half of the twelfth century. It is an official Cistercian manual called the *Usus conversorum,* and contains 22 chapters.[20] To this a monk of Clairvaux added the *Regula conversorum* containing 16 chapters. This *Regula* says expressly that it is supplementary to the *Usus,* and it dates from after 1174, the year in which St. Bernard was canonized, for it refers to him with the term "*Sanctus.*" [21]

Since the purpose of the *conversi,* though these were not to take over the manual labor of the monks altogether,[22] was nevertheless to supplement whatever the monks could not themselves do compatibly with their Benedictine life, these rules consider the lay brothers primarily as laborers. Only those who gave promise of being useful on the farms or in the monastery shops were received. They had a six months' postulancy before

---

[19] Knowles, *The Monastic Order in England,* p. 634.

[20] Hoffmann, *Das Konverseninstitut,* p. 48. Cf. Guignard, *Les monuments,* pp. 276–287, where it is included in the *Consuetudines* which received papal approval on December 23, 1119; Paris-Séjalon, *Nomasticòn Cisterciense* (2. ed., Solesmis, 1892), pp. 235–241.

[21] Martène-Durand, *Thesaurus Novus Anecdotorum* (5 vols., Lutetiae Parisiorum, 1717), IV, 1647 sq. To be cited as *Thesaurus.*

[22] *Exordium parvum,* c. 15; *Consuetudines Ordinis Cisterciensis,* c. 75, de labore, and c. 84, de tempore secationis et messionis—Guignard, *Les monuments,* pp. 61, 177, 190. The monks of Cluny made fun of the manual labor of the Cistercians: "What kind of a monastery is it where the monks dig in the earth, cut down trees, haul manure?"—St. Bernard, *Epistolae—MPL,* CLXXXII, 73.

their novitiate year, and were not clothed as novices until they had proved they could work. It is expressly stated that every *conversus* had to do the work of at least one hired hand.[23]

For this reason the *conversi* vocations were drawn preferably from among the working classes: the sons of farmers, laborers and artisans, who were used to such toil. The general chapter of 1188 even forbade abbots to admit educated men as *conversi*, but specified that they were to be taken as monks.[24]

Inasmuch as the *conversi* were primarily laborers, their prayers were shorter than those of the monks, their office consisting of 20 Our Fathers and *Gloria Patris* for Matins (40 on feasts of 12 lessons), 10 for Lauds, and 5 for each of the other hours. They went to confession every week and communicated seven times a year. Their fasts were less strenuous than those of the monks, and their cloister was not as strict, though there were the most stringent rules regarding their converse with women.[25]

The *conversi* were truly religious, though not monks,[26] and after their postulancy and novitiate they made before the abbot a solemn[27] vow of obedience until death, a vow including those of poverty and chastity. They wore a habit different from that of the monks, and delinquent lay brothers were threatened with penalties analogous to those inflicted for infractions by the monks.[28]

To assure the permanence of the institute of lay brothers, and thus the lasting success of the Cistercian reform, the unconditional subordination of the *conversi* to the monks and the strictest separation between the two classes was found necessary. Thus

---

[23] Martène-Durand, *Thesaurus*, IV, 1327, n. 2, 1338, n. 1.

[24] *Ibid.*, p. 1263, n. 4.

[25] *Inst. Cap. Gen. collecta anno 1134*, c. 7—Guignard, *Les monuments*, p. 251; *Usus conversorum*, c. 7—Martène-Durand, *Thesaurus*, IV, 1251, n. 58; 1252, n. 13.

[26] *Exordium parvum*, c. 15; *Usus conversorum*, c. 13.

[27] Benedictus XIV, decr. 21 mart. 1747—Bizzarri, *Collectanea in usum Secretariae S. C. Episcoporum et Regularium* (Romae, 1863), pp. 407–409. This collection will be cited as Bizzarri, *Coll. S. C. Ep. et Reg.*

[28] *Usus conversorum*, cc. 12, 13—Martène-Durand, *Thesaurus*, IV, 1267, n. 13; 1310, n. 4; 1349, n. 11.

a *conversus* was never allowed to become a monk, and once a novice took the habit of a lay brother every hope of this kind was cut off. If a lay brother left the Cistercians and became a monk or canon regular, he had to come back and be a *conversus,* unless he had received Orders, in which case he was not to be received back.[29]

The abbot of Chalis disobeyed this law and promoted one of his lay brothers, a gifted man by the name of Lambert, to the rank of monk. The general chapter assembled at Citeaux in 1237 summarily ordered the abbot to dismiss Lambert and not to receive him back into the monastery except as a *conversus,* and on condition that he show due repentance for his transgression.[30]

On the contrary, monks who wanted to become *conversi* were also subject to strict regulations. When such a one was in sacred Orders and received this permission, he had to continue to wear the tonsure. Priests and clerics who wanted to become *conversi* out of humility were forbidden to do so, in order that the class distinction could be maintained.[31]

The *conversi* were of course not admitted to the monks' chapter, and they were formally denied any voice in the election of the abbot by the general chapter in 1181, apparently because they had proved themselves trouble-makers.[32]

A means of keeping the *conversi* in their auxiliary position was the prohibition of any education or intellectual pursuit. Their whole education was a weekly instruction in religion, and they were forbidden to learn to read or write.

> They may not have a book nor may they learn anything but the Our Father, the Creed, the *Miserere,* and such prayers as they have to know by heart.[33]

This was not taken amiss by the *conversi* of those days, for they and their people were used to illiteracy as the normal thing.

---

29 *Usus conversorum,* c. 13.

30 Martène-Durand, *Thesaurus,* IV, 1365, n. 11. The first dispensation occurred in the year 1397.—*Ibid.,* IV, 1534, n. 2.

31 *Ibid.,* p. 1316, n. 19.

32 *Usus conversorum,* c. 11—Martène-Durand, *op. cit.,* IV, 1253, n. 2.

33 *Usus conversorum,* c. 9.

Partly because they were denied the education to fit them for competent administration, and especially with a view to keeping them under control,[34] the *conversi* came to be placed under the cellarer of the monastery in their daily work. The lay brothers continued, however, as the heads of the various granges,[35] and thus were themselves immediately responsible for the work done in their own departments.

Under this Cistercian régime the lay brother institute achieved its greatest success, as its monastic purpose of enabling the monks to lead their proper religious life was firmly supported by the contemporary secular situation of feudal class distinctions in society as a whole. The Cistercians recruited their *conversi* from among the bondmen or serfs, and, abolishing every distinction between bondmen and free,[36] made them free men who like the monks enjoyed all the immunities and privileges of a powerful order.[37]

This very sociological fact, however, became one of the reasons for the decline of the institute, inasmuch as it encouraged the lower classes in their struggle for liberty and equality. For, as Boyd notes:[38]

> But as early as the beginning of the thirteenth century the peasants of many regions were discovering that

[34] Hurter, *Geschichte Papst Innocenz' III und seiner Zeitgenossen* (4 vols., Hamburg, 1844), II, 70 sq. The lay brothers of Grammont (Flanders) had taken over the material possessions of the monastery. They were a scandal to all Christendom and caused trouble for ten popes in their repeated rebellions against their superiors and their struggle for the control of their monastery.

[35] Knowles, *The Monastic Order in England,* p. 633.

[36] St. Benedict, *Rule,* c. 2.

[37] Henry I (1126–1181), Count of Champagne (1152–1181), in the year 1164 gave his serfs general permission to enter the Cistercian Abbey of Le Reclus. Cf. Hoffmann, *Das Konverseninstitut,* p. 5; Vacandard, *Vie de St. Bernard* (2 vols., Paris, 1895), I, 445. There can be little doubt that other noblemen did the same, as they invited the Cistercians to occupy their lands, and helped them in every possible way.

[38] *A Cistercian Nunnery in Mediaeval Italy—The Story of Rifreddo in Saluzzo, 1220–1300,* Harvard Historical Monographs, XVIII (Cambridge, Massachusetts: Harvard University Press, 1943), p. 164. To be cited as *A Cistercian Nunnery.*

the free air of the towns was more congenial than the silence of the Cistercian granges, and a shortage of lay-brothers soon made itself felt, necessitating a modification of the strict prohibition upon leasing Cistercian property to lay cultivators.

## §3. Adaptations of the Cistercian "Conversi" Institute in Other Orders

The Cistercian model was not an isolated phenomenon, but it portrayed the lay brother institute in its full development. It inspired much of the legislation of the Canons Regular [39] and the Carthusians. According to Knowles: [40]

> The Charterhouse had from early days a clear conception of the functions of its lay brethren which combined the ideas of Vallombrosa and Citeaux. The *conversi* existed to cultivate the land and to perform all the heavy manual tasks in order to safeguard the seclusion of the monks; they were never permitted to grow beyond a fixed number or to occupy responsible administrative positions; at the same time their life was fully recognized as a vocation, and was carefully regulated on lines similar to those of the monks, but with a more cenobitic complexion. In the early days of the order they had cells, offices and oratory wholly separate from those of the monks, and closely connected with the quarters of the guests, and the first Charterhouses . . . consisted of an "upper" and a "lower" house, the terms being adopted from the mother-house of the Chartreuse.[41]

St. Dominic (1170–1221) adopted the same fundamental principles when he founded his great order, with this modification that, instead of enabling monks to live according to their rule, the function of the Dominican brothers was to relieve their

---

[39] Cf. *Constitutiones Praemonstratensium* and *Consuetudines Canonicorum Regularium S. Victoris Parisiensis*—Martène, *De Antiquis Ecclesiae Ritibus* (Ed. novissima, 4 vols., Antuaerpiae-Venetiis, 1763-1764), III, 323 sq.; 741 sq.

[40] *The Monastic Order in England*, pp. 378–379.

[41] Cf. Deroux, *Les Origines*, pp. 125–126.

clerical confrères of such tasks and cares as would hinder them in their apostolic work.[42]

A few years earlier St. Francis of Assisi (1182–1226) had gone against the class distinction current in the society of his time, and placed his friars all on the same plane, after the manner of the monks according to St. Benedict's *Rule*.[43]

Smet, writing on "The Origin of the Carmelite Laybrothers," has given a splendid summary of the life and work of the mendicant *conversi:* [44]

> The Mendicant Friar had need of someone to care for his convents, poor and small though they were. He also had need of an aide in his preaching tours. The laybrother accompanied the friar on his journeys, and did the household tasks about the convent. Not the least of his services was the assistance of his prayers and good works. The position of the laybrother in the new Mendicant Orders, and his relation to the cleric, is admirably summed up in the well-known picture of the friar preaching to the people, while at the base of the pulpit is seated a laybrother recollectedly fingering his beads. . . .
>
> In the long run, therefore, the Mendicant Orders ended by setting up the Laybrotherhood as an institute subordinate to the clerical state. It must be noted, however, that though, in the new order, the laybrother occupies a position inferior to that of the priest, from the point of view of jurisdictional rights, he is nevertheless as much a member of the Order as the cleric. In the old monastic system the Laybrotherhood formed a separate institute apart from the monastic state, lay and cleric. Among the Mendicant Orders it constitutes a lay element in the very bosom of the Order. . . . If wise experience dictated the measure of eliminating the laybrother from administrative and legislative posts, it was not in order to cut him off from the life of the Order, but to spare him labors for which by his training he was not qualified. It is a matter of vocation. . . .

---

[42] Mulhern, *The Early Dominican Laybrother*, pp. 21–24; 67–88.

[43] St. Francis, *Rule*, cc. 7, 9; St. Benedict, *Rule*, cc. 2, 3, 21, 31, 35, 60, 62, 63.

[44] *The Sword* (Englewood, N. J.–Washington, D. C., 1937–), VI (1942), 129, 131.

The lay brother institute has been found in a number of instances attached to communities of women religious, for, "The rule of enclosure involved the presence of laybrothers and lay-sisters to discharge the business of the nunnery which lay outside the convent walls." [45]

The religious societies and congregations founded since the thirteenth century have made varying use of the lay brother institute, adopting it wholly or in part, and adapting it to their own particular needs. The old orders too have made changes from time to time, especially as their work began to overlap, sometimes borrowing from other communities elements that had formerly been the factors of differentiation.

---

[45] Boyd, *A Cistercian Nunnery,* p. 109; cf. also Knowles, *The Monastic Order in England,* pp. 204, 206.

# CHAPTER III

## THE CHURCH'S GENERAL LAW FOR *CONVERSI* BEFORE THE CODE

In the study of the *conversi* institute one cannot draw general conclusions from particular legislation, for there is, in fact, no homogeneous "*conversi* institute." The term *conversi* has been applied through the past centuries to many classes of men, from religious with solemn vows, down the gamut of *sodales* with simple vows or with but the single vow of obedience, to mere lay servants employed in religious houses. So it was true to say with Wolter[1] that the *conversi* made simple vows, as long as the statement was interpreted to include only *some conversi;* and it was also true to say that *conversi* were not religious,[2] provided that this statement too applied only to *some,* and *not* to *all, conversi.* Holy Mother Church, in her universal solicitude, has made salutary laws for all these persons.

### §1. Some "Conversi" Always Admitted to Solemn Vows

Although the Church never prohibited *conversi* in general from making solemn vows, there grew up in the eighteenth century a jurisprudence which questioned the solemnity of the Cistercian *conversi's* vows so seriously as to justify the personal intervention of the *princeps canonistarum.* The decree of Pope Benedict XIV, dated March 21, 1747, is sufficiently important and informative to justify quotation at length:[3]

> Having consulted with a special commission deputed for the purpose and consisting of the Cardinals de Gentilibus, Cavalchini, Tamburini and Besozzi, as also the Archbishop Damascene, of the Congregation of

[1] *Praecipua Elementa,* pp. 485, 515.

[2] *Guidonis Papae I Decisiones* (Ed. Gasparis Baronis, Genevae, 1643), p. 528, q. 563, 5.

[3] Bizzarri, *Coll. S. C. Ep. et Reg.,* pp. 407–409.

Bishops and Regulars . . . on the *dubium:* "Whether the vows pronounced by Cistercian *conversi* are simple or solemn?"

When the controversy as to whether the vows made by Cistercian *conversi* were simple or solemn was brought to the *Signatura* of the Apostolic Penitentiary, this body declined to settle the question, giving as its reason that it should be investigated by the Congregation of Bishops and Regulars, which had already received the representations of the Fathers General and Procurator General of the Cistercian Order.

But since no decision has so far been forthcoming from this Congregation either, We deemed it fitting and proper to take the whole affair into our own hands and to examine it thoroughly with the help of a special commission, consisting of the above named Cardinals and Archbishop whom We appointed. When this investigation was made in our presence on the sixteenth day of the current month of March, the commission decided by unanimous vote that the vows made by Cistercian *conversi* were not simple but solemn.

And certainly, since from the very beginnings of the Cistercian Order in the eleventh century *conversi* were joined to the monks, in order that these latter could give themselves to solitude and contemplation in the cloister, and the *conversi* should have charge of those departments which took care of the necessaries of life, and it was laid down concerning them that "they decided to take lay *conversi barbati* with the permission of their bishop, and to treat them in life and in death like themselves in everything, except that they should not become monks"[4] . . . ; since it was decreed in the II Lateran Council held in 1139 under Pope Innocent II, that the marriages of *conversi* who had made their religious profession were null;[5] since this was confirmed in the Council of Rheims (1147),[6] held under Pope Eugene III, who had been abbot of Saints Vincent and Anastasius at Rome *ad aquas Salvias,* and who was a pupil of St. Bernard; since Pope Alexander III in his

[4] *Exordium parvum,* c. 15—Guignard, *Les monuments,* p. 61.

[5] C. 40, C. XXVII, q. 1.

[6] Can. 7—Mansi, *Sacrorum Conciliorum Nova et Amplissima Collectio* (53 vols. in 60, Paris-Leipzig-Arnhem, 1901–1927), XXI, 715. This collection will be cited as Mansi.

decretal which begins *Non est vobis*[7] declared that both monks and *conversi* of the Cistercian order are bound by an equal obligation of obedience to their abbot; all these indicate that the vows made by Cistercian *conversi* are not simple but solemn. This was also noted by Mabillon, who was very well versed regarding monastic institutions, in his preface to part 2, sixth century, *Ordinis S. Benedicti*, §11. Likewise no solid reason against this opinion is to be found in the wording of the profession formula of the Cistercian *conversi:* "Father, I promise you obedience *de bono* until death." For, besides, it is certain that in the first five Christian centuries no set form of words was prescribed for making profession, and not even according to the present discipline does the profession formula of one regular institute correspond to that of another, since the disciples of St. Benedict promise local stability, conversion of manners, and obedience according to the rule of St. Benedict; the sons of St. Dominic vow obedience according to the rule of St. Augustine; the followers of St. Bruno promise conversion of their manners; which promise seems equivalent to that of the Cistercian *conversi*, obedience *de bono* until death.

The force of the present argument is derived not only from a consideration of the words but also of the other extrinsic circumstances. In the book of ancient definitions of the Cistercian order, Dist. XIV, cap. 1, tit. *de receptione, et professione Conversorum,* we read that upon completing his year of novitiate the *conversus* approaches the monks' chapter, where he prostrates himself on the ground, rises at the command of the abbot, and, having been questioned, promises his stability. After this the abbot says, "Det tibi Deus perseverantiam;" and all answer, "Amen." Then, having renounced all ownership, distributing his goods to whomsoever he wishes but preferably to the poor, he kneels down, joins his hands and places them between the hands of the abbot, and promises him obedience *de bono* until death. The abbot says, "Det tibi Deus vitam aeternam;" and all answer, "Amen." . . .

The approach to the chapter, not before or during the novitiate, but upon its completion at the end of a year, the promise of stability after being asked concerning it, and its acceptance by the abbot, who has the right to

[7] C. 7, X, *de regularibus et transeuntibus ad religionem,* III, 31.

receive the profession, the solemn abdication of property, the kneeling before the abbot and the other ceremonies that accompany the promise of obedience *de bono* until death, the petition for eternal life in answer to the promise of obedience, give sufficient indication that the profession is solemn, and in it are implicitly and virtually contained the vows of chastity, poverty and obedience, which, since they are made in a regular profession, are not simple but solemn, according to the reply of Boniface VIII in the one chapter *de voto, et voti redemptione,* in Sexto.

The unanimous vote of the commission in favor of the solemnity of the vows of the Cistercian *conversi* was approved by Us orally at the session itself. This decision is confirmed by Us in this our present decree . . . so that in the future there will be unanimous recognition of the solemnity of the vows of the Cistercian *conversi.*

This decision of Pope Benedict XIV was no innovation, nor did it single out the Cistercians as an exceptional case. Forty-four years earlier the Sacred Congregation of Bishops and Regulars had answered three questions of the Bishop of Grenoble regarding the *conversae* of the monastery of St. Clare in that city as follows: [8]

1. Are the *conversae* of the order religious?

Ans. These *conversae* are true religious bound by the four solemn vows of poverty, chastity, obedience and perpetual cloister, like the other nuns of the monastery in question.

2. If they are religious, are they to wear the black veil like the choir nuns and like them also have a voice in the chapter?

Ans. Nothing is to be changed regarding the white veil, which all *conversae* wear to distinguish them from the choir sisters, not only in the order in question, but in the other orders of St. Ursula, the B. V. M. and Sts. Benedict and Bernardine; nor do the *conversae* have a voice in the chapter, just as those of the other orders mentioned have none.

3. Are the *conversae* bound to observe the fasts, prostrations on the ground, and choir offices, notwith-

[8] July, 1703—Bizzarri, *Coll. S. C. Ep. et Reg.*, p. 318.

standing the labor and tasks it is their duty to perform for the whole community, especially since these *conversae* pronounce their vows according to the same formula used by the other sisters?

Ans. It is left to the prudence and discretion of the local bishop to dispense these *conversae* from the more difficult observances mentioned, or to leave the matter to the abbess or superior, who upon examining the case should with kindness mitigate these observances for the *conversae,* in consideration of the work and most difficult tasks they have to do for the other sisters and the whole community.[9]

That the institute of *conversi* professed with solemn vows continued until the time of the Code is witnessed by the decree of March 19, 1857, of the Sacred Congregation of Bishops and Regulars,[10] and the decree *Sacrosancta,* issued by the Sacred Congregation for Religious on January 1, 1911.[11]

## §2. Some "Conversi" Restricted to Taking Simple Vows and Others to not Taking Any Vows at All

In the very laws in which the Church recognized *conversi* as religious with solemn vows, she often laid down such stringent requirements, especially with regard to the minimum age for profession,[12] that it became more expedient for religious orders and congregations to have their constitutions restrict them to the

[9] It is important to note in the last question and answer of this response that the profession formula has no influence in determining the status of *conversi.* This formula has always been left entirely to the particular legislation of the various religious institutes. Cf. can. 576, §1; Schaefer, *De Religiosis ad normam Codicis Iuris Canonici* (3. ed., Romae, 1940), n. 266, 5. To be cited as *De Religiosis.* The status of the *conversi* is determined solely by their constitutions.

[10] *Codicis Iuris Canonici Fontes cura Emi Petri Card. Gasparri editi* (9 vols., Romae, postea Civitate Vaticana: Typis Polyglottis Vaticanis, 1923–1939. Vols. VII–IX ed. cura et studio Emi Iustiniani Card. Serédi), n. 1976. This collection will be cited as *Fontes.*

[11] *Fontes,* n. 4407.

[12] Pope Clement VIII prescribed the completion of the twenty-first year. —Const. *Cum ad regularem,* 19 mart. 1603, §16—*Fontes,* n. 189. The completion of the thirtieth year was required by the decree *Sacrosancta* of the Sacred Congregation for Religious on January 1, 1911—*Fontes,* n. 4407.

taking of simple vows.[13] This limitation to the taking of simple vows was a serious blow to the *conversi* institute in pre-Code law, inasmuch as persons with only simple vows, except the Jesuits,[14] were not considered canonical religious prior to the time of Pope Leo XIII,[15] and members of congregations of simple vows were denied the name and privileges of religious, unless they had obtained these grants by special indult, up to the time of the Code.[16]

The injustice of robbing the *conversi* of their status as full-fledged religious, which they had vindicated for themselves for seven centuries, was too obvious to escape notice. But instead of restoring solemn vows for them, which in the nineteenth century came to be safeguarded by difficult canonical requirements,[17] their religious orders sponsored a new jurisprudence, contrary to the law of the Church at that time, which anomalously called the *conversi* "true religious of simple vows." [18] This trend gathered strength rapidly, for it is witnessed in the decree *Ecclesia catholica* issued by the Sacred Congregation of Bishops and Regulars [19] little more than three decades after its decree

---

[13] Thus the Calced Carmelites and Beuronese Benedictines.—Molitor, *Religiosi Iuris Capita Selecta* (Ratisbonae, 1909), p. 173. To be cited as *Capita Selecta.*

[14] Gregorius XIII, const. *Quanto fructuosius,* 1 febr. 1583, §5—*Fontes,* n 150; const. *Ascendente Domino,* 25 maii 1584—*Fontes,* n. 153.

[15] S. C. Ep. et Reg., *Cenomanen.,* 19 apr. 1844—*Fontes,* n. 1938. Cf. Bizzarri, *Coll. S. C. Ep. et Reg.* (ed. 1885), p. 745, nota. This is the only citation from Bizzarri's 1885 edition in the present dissertation. All other quotations are from the 1863 edition.

[16] Benedictus XIV, const. *Quamvis iusto,* 30 apr. 1749, §13—*Fontes,* n. 398. Cf. Larraona, "Commentarium,"—*Commentarium pro Religiosis* (Romae, 1920–; ab anno 1935: *Commentarium pro Religiosis et Missionariis*), I (1920), 46, n. 2. The *Commentarium* will be cited as *CpR* and, for issues since 1935, *CpRM.*

[17] S. C. super Statu Regularium, litt. encycl. *Neminem latet,* 19 mart. 1857—*Fontes,* n. 4381; S. C. Ep. et Reg., decr. 19 mart. 1857—*Fontes,* n. 1976.

[18] Thus Wolter, *Praecipua Elementa,* pp. 485, 515.

[19] 11 aug. 1889—*Acta Sanctae Sedis* (Romae, 1865–1908, declared the Holy See's authentic and official periodical by Pope Pius X, May 23, 1904), XXIII (1890–1891), 634–636. This periodical will be cited as *ASS.*

requiring three years in simple vows before admission to solemn profession. The decree *Ecclesia catholica* indicated broad exceptions to the traditional strict law when it spoke of " formal or true religious congregations of simple vows " at a time previous to Pope Leo XIII's Constitution *Conditae a Christo,*[20] the " Magna Carta " of simple vow religious congregations.[21] Thus the *conversi* with simple vows who were conceded to be religious before the Code foreshadowed those who were to be guaranteed full canonical status as religious under the new dispensation. Concessions are at times odious however, and many lay brothers suffered by their limitation to the taking of simple vows before 1918.

Two constitutions of Pope Sixtus V (1585–1590) are important in this regard, as in the first the Pontiff spoke of *conversi* who were mere servants according to the laws of their monasteries and were not to be admitted to profession, whereas in the second, which was issued as an authentic explanation of the first, he spoke of *conversi* who were truly religious, and mentioned the conditions to be verified before they were to be admitted to vows. The first constitution, *Cum de omnibus,* dated November 26, 1587, reads in part as follows: [22]

> While our most important duty is to preserve all the degrees of ecclesiastical orders in fitting purity and worthiness, our chief solicitude is to ward off as far as possible every stain of sin and shame and every occasion of scandal from communities of regulars who, since they are dedicated to God, ought to shine with the highest luster and holiness. Since the very nature of the thing warns us how disgraceful it would be, and how lacking in the respect due to the divine majesty and to the persons consecrated to God, if a certain type of men, fearing the justice of secular criminal courts because of their own crimes, or branded with perpetual ignominy and excluded from both honor and inheritance because of the shame and sin in which they were born, should

[20] 8 dec. 1900—*Fontes,* n. 644.

[21] Schaefer, *De Religiosis,* n. 67. Cf. also Molitor, *Capita Selecta,* pp. 170 sq.

[22] *Fontes,* n. 162.

be offered as victims to almighty God and admitted indiscriminately to live in the house of honor and holiness with those who minister to the Lord (to serve whom is to reign) and take part in sacred functions far nobler than any worldly pre-eminence. . . .

§1. Let it not come to pass therefore that bastards, who as a rule imitate the vice and incontinency of their parents, and who run to a monastery not for the love of God but for the comforts of this life (since they are debarred from the inheritances of their parents and the more honorable professions), should, most likely in a disgraceful manner and to the loss of their souls, lead a life in religion which they would begin with a wrong intention and continue against the laws of the order; let them not by their corrupt morals and bad example disturb the peace and tranquillity of the others who serve God, and let not this scum of the earth and rabble drag the honor and reputation of religious communities so low as to offer them as asylums for illegitimate children, and so encourage promiscuous persons in their propensity, but let these last be rather deterred from indulging their carnal passions when they see that this refuge is no longer open to their offspring.

§2. By this our present constitution to hold for all time we strictly interdict and forbid those who are illegitimate by reason of incest or sacrilege, . . . from entering a monastery of any order whatsoever, mendicant or non-mendicant, whether of brethren, monks, hermits, canons or clerics regular, of congregations or of hospitalers, or from being granted the habit or profession as regulars, or from being admitted in any way whatsoever. . . . But lest the way be closed entirely to those who desire in a spirit of humility to serve God and religion and to do penance in a monastery or house of regulars, we permit the above indicated persons who are illegitimate by reason of incest or sacrilege to be admitted to the habit of *conversi* or of servants employed in monasteries or houses of regulars, where they may be allowed to do servile work and the meaner tasks and labors, *on this condition,* however, *that they be perpetually estopped and barred from receiving the religious habit or from making profession,* and from minor as well as major orders, as well as from the clerical state and all ecclesiastical offices, functions and dignities.[23]

[23] Italics inserted by the present writer.

The second constitution, *Ad Romanum,* which appeared the following year, on October 21, 1588, thus interpreted the law just cited:[24]

> §12. As to the profession of the illegitimate and those who have received the regular habit after the completion of their sixteenth year, since they are really and truly to be considered religious only after having made profession, we decree that those who received the habit prior to the publication of our aforementioned constitution and desire to make profession after its promulgation, are not to be admitted thereto before investigations have been made and the form has been observed as it is prescribed in the constitution; and the profession of those who since its promulgation have been admitted without the requisite investigation is null and void if the form has not been kept, even through ignorance. But among oblates and *conversi* who make their profession it is enough that an investigation be made regarding their moral habits and their personal status. . . .
>
> §18. For the rest, the prescriptions we laid down in the aforesaid constitution for male religious are not by any means to be extended to nuns at this time.

Three years later, Pope Gregory XIV, the second successor of Sixtus V, mitigated the legislation of the constitutions just cited to such an extent that the laws they contained were practically abrogated.[25]

Although it may appear that Pope Sixtus V in his two constitutions considered the *conversi* an inferior kind of religious, it must be noted that in the first document he did not regard them as religious at all. The *Cum de omnibus* spoke of *conversi* who were mere servants about the monastery, and not religious. The prohibition of the constitution, namely that those who were illegitimate by reason of incest or sacrilege "be perpetually estopped and barred from receiving the religious habit or from making profession" applied with full force to the *conversi* in monasteries which had them at that time as true religious. The

---

[24] *Fontes,* n. 164.

[25] Const. *Circumspecta,* 15 mart. 1591—*Fontes,* n. 170.

reason the second constitution could dispense with the formal investigation in the case of *conversi* was that the seculars who were causing the trouble were not interested in becoming laboring brothers.

The injury to the prestige of the *conversi* inferred from the *Cum de omnibus* was that it mentioned a species of *conversi* who were not religious but servants. The *Ad Romanum* dispensed in the case of oblates and *conversi* from the formalities requisite for the valid reception of other religious, but made no discrimination regarding the actual qualities required for admission to these auxiliary classes.

The decline of monasticism from its positive ideals was the reason why the *conversi* fell from their high religious status to the low position of serfs. In many places nobility of birth became one of the requisites for admission to a monastery as a "monk." In consequence of secular influence membership in the capacity of a monk in a monastery had become a prebendal office with a fixed income. Only those who were of noble birth could be admitted to this form of social security, whereas serfs desiring to embrace the religious life retained their lowly status and entered the monastery as *conversi*. Hilpisch sees in these circumstances the reason for the downfall of monasticism in the fifteenth century.[26]

## §3. Relations of "Conversi" to Clerics and Other Religious; Transfer between Classes

The Church has always encouraged religious vocations of every kind. The time of a flourishing lay monasticism, however, was relatively short; good monks soon proved themselves good clerics. The cleavage that resulted between the clerical and lay members of religious institutes is founded on the Church's divinely established constitutional hierarchy,[27] and has and will always create problems for ecclesiastical legislation. This basic division has

[26] *Geschichte des benediktinischen Mönchtums* (Freiburg im Breisgau: Herder, 1929), p. 254. Cf. Linneborn, *Der Zustand der westfälischen Benediktinerklöster in den letzten 50 Jahren vor ihrem Anschluss an die Bursfelder Kongregation* (Münster, 1898), pp. 3 sq.

[27] Cf. can. 108, §3.

been aggravated by the incidental distinctions based on birth, education and talent, which have complicated the relations of the various classes in the same communities, and have required different and changing legislation to meet new difficulties as they arose.[28]

The earliest general Church law which excluded lay religious from one of the legal rights of their clerical confrères was a decretal of Pope Boniface VIII (1294–1303): [29]

> . . . In churches of regulars and in monasteries those who are not tacitly or expressly professed are not to take part with the professed in elections, nor are lay brothers to take part with clerics.

Pope Clement VIII (1592–1605) in his Constitution *Cum ad regularem*[30] forbade regular *conversi* to transfer to the clerical class even during their time of probation. An apostolic indult was therefore necessary for this change. Lucius Ferraris (+ ca. 1763)[31] cited Donatus (+ 1661) as saying[32] that the reason for this prohibition was the removal of ready occasions for troublesome ambition. He also cited subsequent decrees of the Holy See which prescribed that superiors should be suspended from their office if they admitted *conversi* to holy Orders; that those so ordained were to be perpetually suspended from the exercise of the Orders received; that a *conversus* who lawfully transferred to the clerical state should reckon his seniority from the time of the transfer, and not from the beginning of his religious life as a lay brother.

The opposite transfer, however, from the clerical to the lay class of religious, was not forbidden. This change could be

---

[28] Cf. Suarez, *Tractatus de Religione Societatis Jesu* (ed. De Reverseaux, Bruxellis-Parisiis, 1857), lib. VII, cc. 1, 3.

[29] C. 32, *de electione et electi potestate,* I, 6, in VI°.

[30] 19 mart. 1603, §16—*Fontes,* n. 189.

[31] *Prompta Bibliotheca, Canonica, Iuridica, Moralis, Theologica, nec non Ascetica, Polemica, Rubricistica, Historica* (8 vols., Romae, 1766), s. v. *transitus,* n. 5.

[32] *Rerum Regularium Praxis Resolutoria* (4 vols., Coloniae Agrippinae, 1675), tom. II, tract. XIV, q. 14.

made "for a just cause with only the permission of the regular superior, either the provincial or the general, with the consent of his counsellors, or in any other manner prescribed by the statutes of the order, provided that the one who transferred was not in holy Orders . . . Sanchez (1550–1610) and Cardinal Petra (1662–1747) state that the regular superior can not only permit such a transfer, but can even command it in punishment for a crime. But I should think it more prudent in these cases to refer the matter to the Apostolic See." [33] It was disputed whether the permission of the Holy See was needed in the case of the transfer of nuns from one class to another.

In its *animadversiones* on June 9, 1860, on the Constitutions of the Sisters of St. Joseph in the diocese of Chambéry, the Sacred Congregation of Bishops and Regulars noted (n. 12): "It is a dangerous innovation to permit *conversae* to pass to the class of choir sisters." [34] Finally, article 50 of the *Normae* of the same Sacred Congregation, published in 1901, forbade the transfer from one class to another in all new congregations with simple vows.

The Sacred Congregation of Bishops and Regulars warned against too sharp a distinction between the various classes of religious, in its *animadversiones* on the constitutions of a congregation of priests under the title of the Immaculate Conception of the Blessed Virgin Mary: [35]

> Such discrimination between the priests and lay brothers is made in the constitutions that they would constitute two communities rather than one. . . . What is prescribed regarding different classes of meals is contrary to the customs of other institutes, presents difficulty and danger in practice, and militates against the mutual fraternal charity which the members of the same community are bound to show to one another, even though their status is different.

---

[33] Ferraris, *loc. cit.*, n. 9; Bouix, *Tractatus de Jure Regularium* (2 vols., Parisiis, 1857), II, 534–535.

[34] Bizzarri, *Coll. S. C. Ep. et Reg.*, p. 838.

[35] 2 mart. 1861, ad 4um—Bizzarri, *Coll. S. C. Ep. et Reg.*, p. 845.

## §4. The "Cum ad regularem," "Neminem latet," and "Sacrosancta"

The most noteworthy characteristic of the Church's legislation for *conversi* is that at least from the time of the Council of Trent she has officially considered their status and vocation most difficult to human nature, and a most austere calling in the religious life. She has retained the ancient principle of the decretals, that youths are not to be admitted to the more difficult and austere monasteries until they are somewhat advanced in years and maturity,[36] and thus it is that in all her pre-Code legislation from the time of Pope Clement VIII's Constitution *Cum ad regularem* the chief emphasis has been placed upon a required minimum age, however strange this stress on that particular point may seem in view of the apparently greater relative value of other matters in the law for *conversi*. The minimum age was advanced gradually until the Sacred Congregation for Religious decreed on January 1, 1911, that lay brothers were not to be admitted to solemn vows until they had completed their thirtieth year.[37]

The early seventeenth century was a time of great concern on the part of the Church's supreme legislators for non-clerical religious. A whole body of law for *conversi* was built upon Pope Clement VIII's Constitution *Cum ad regularem,* issued on March 19, 1603.[38] Extracts from this Constitution are given here:

> §4. Whoever desires to be received into a Regular Order, including the Mendicants, must be of the age prescribed by the rules and constitutions of the respective society; besides this he must have the required education, or at least give good proof that he is able to learn what is necessary for admission to minor Orders, and later on to major Orders, according to the decrees of the Council of Trent. But if anyone is more than twenty-five years old and desires to enter a Regular

[36] C. 6, X, *de regularibus et transeuntibus ad religionem,* III, 31.

[37] Decr. *Sacrosancta—Fontes,* n. 4407. This was abrogated by the Code in canons 573 and 574.—S. C. de Religiosis, 6 oct. 1919—*Acta Apostolicae Sedis, Commentarium Officiale* (Romae, 1909–), XI (1919), 420. To be cited as *AAS.*

[38] *Fontes,* n. 189.

Order, and at the same time does not have the required schooling, he is to be admitted only among the *conversi*, who do not need this training. Lay brothers, however, are not to be received until they are twenty years old, and not unless they know at least the principal elements of Christian doctrine.

§5. [The superiors] are to take care that all candidates, including *conversi*, be instructed, by those whose duty it is, regarding the rule they are to profess, the three essential vows, the religious state, and the particular regulations and constitutions of the respective Order, before they are admitted to the regular habit. . . .

§15. Although the education of the clerics should have the first place in the monastery, the religious instruction of the *conversi* is not to be neglected. This training is rather to be pursued in the same way, for it has been sufficiently demonstrated that, since the lay brothers profess the same rule, their perfect education brings honor and glory to the religious state, and gives a useful and edifying example to the faithful. The *conversi* shall be assigned a place for sleeping apart from the novitiate of the clerics (insofar as this can be conveniently arranged). Notwithstanding this separation, however, they are to be subject to and obey the novice master and the superiors of the monastery, according to the statutes and constitutions of the respective Order. These superiors in turn shall not only try them out and assign them to manual tasks, but shall also, according to their ability and convenience, diligently instruct them in spiritual things, especially as to the manner of mental prayer, and to this end the lay brothers are to be summoned, whenever that be possible, to the chapters and spiritual conferences held by the novice masters, and they are to meet in church at stated times, unless they are actually occupied elsewhere at their various tasks.

§16. At the end of the time of probation only those who have been found by a new and thorough examination not only to be capable of religious perfection but also to be fit for manual labor (provided that the clerics have completed their sixteenth year, and the *conversi* their twenty-first) are to be admitted to profession. Those who have been received as *conversi* can never pass to the clerical state, even during their time of probation.

The Sacred Congregation of Bishops and Regulars applied §16 in two specific cases not long after the Constitution was promulgated.[39] In a decree dated September 21, 1624, the Sacred Congregation of the Council renewed the whole Constitution *Cum ad regularem.*[40]

With the defection of many from the religious state after they had made solemn vows, the Church was compelled about the middle of the nineteenth century to introduce a new law to provide all candidates for this state with a longer time for deliberation before they made their final profession. This new law, made for all orders with solemn vows, and therefore binding upon *conversi,* prescribed a previous three year period in simple vows for all candidates who aspired to solemn profession. The decree, which was an excerpt from the encyclical *Neminem latet* issued by the Sacred Congregation *super statu Regularium* on March 19, 1857,[41] was promulgated on that same day by the Sacred Congregation of Bishops and Regulars:[42]

> . . . Having finished the probation and the novitiate according to the prescriptions of the Council of Trent (Sess. XXV, *de regularibus,* c. 15), the apostolic constitutions, and the statutes of the Order approved by the Holy See, novices shall make simple vows upon completing their sixteenth year, as prescribed by the Council of Trent, or at whatever age may be required by such statutes of an Order as have been approved by the Holy See; and regarding lay brothers and *conversi,* after they have arrived at the age indicated in the Constitution *In supremo* of Clement VIII. If they are found worthy, the professed shall be admitted to solemn vows three years from the day they made their simple profession . . .

Inasmuch as this decree was not everywhere observed, Pope Pius IX (1846–1878) in his Constitution *Ad universalis* on

[39] *Imolen.,* 18 iun. 1613—*Fontes,* n. 1657; *Minorum Provinciae Baeticae,* 14 febr. 1620—*Fontes,* n. 1708.

[40] §1—*Fontes,* n. 2454.

[41] *Fontes,* n. 4381.

[42] *Fontes,* n. 1976.

February 7, 1862,[43] added the sanction of nullity to any and every solemn profession made by anyone who had not previously completed three years in simple vows.

The final pre-Code general legislation for *conversi* was enacted in the decree *Sacrosancta* of the Sacred Congregation for Religious, dated January 1, 1911.[44] This decree deferred the age for the taking of solemn vows on the part of lay brothers to the time when they had completed their thirtieth year. Inasmuch as the decree incorporates a complete exposition of the facts of the situation as seen by the Sacred Congregation, together with a lengthy instruction for *conversi* and their superiors, its canonical parts are here translated in full:

> The holy Church of God has seen fit to permit religious Orders to have solemn vows, so that those observing the evangelical counsels in these Orders should belong to a state more stable in Christian society both in acknowledgment and in effect. The Church admits even those not destined to share in the priesthood of Christ, namely the *conversi* or lay brothers, to these solemn vows.
>
> Since, however, by solemn vows a man is bound to the divine service by a wholly irrevocable, strict and public bond before the Church and all the faithful, it is most fitting that those who have thus pledged themselves to follow forever more closely in the footsteps of Christ persevere faithful to their promise. This is especially to be noted regarding the lay brothers or *conversi*, who cause wonderment and scandal among the faithful when these see them return to the world after solemn profession, engaging in secular affairs like other men, with no further relation to the life they led in religion.
>
> The spirit of the times, however, which unhappily guarantees undue liberty to men, has filtered also into the sacred precincts of the monasteries. This spirit has weakened the good will to persevere along with the desire of leading a humble life, hidden in Christ, such as is demanded of *conversi* in monasteries, especially in those lay brothers who perhaps have entered religion more out of necessity than of their own free will, or

[43] *Fontes,* n. 532.

[44] *Fontes,* n. 4407.

those whom superiors have received without due caution, or those who have abused the gifts God gave them. Holy Mother Church, choosing the lesser evil, has sometimes in her great mercy permitted these to depart. . . .

That the dignity of the vows, then, which also lay brothers promise solemnly, continue to be held in the honor that it deserves in the Church, and in order the better to insure the sacred pledge of a vocation in our most difficult times, this Sacred Congregation, in whose charge rest the affairs of religious societies, has considered the matter most diligently in the Lord upon exploring the reasons and causes, and proposing the means and remedies. It has asked the opinion of the highest superiors of the great Orders and that of many of its consultors. Considering all these things diligently, the Eminent Cardinals of this Congregation in a plenary session on July 29, 1910, decided to lay down certain rules to be observed in the future regarding the admission of lay religious, their incipient training, their subsequent education, and their final pronouncing of vows.

The following rules are therefore to be observed by all religious communities in which solemn vows are taken also by the *conversi*, namely:

1. The superiors general have the faculty to permit provincial superiors in particular cases to receive youths who wish to become lay brothers even when they have not as yet completed their seventeenth year. All other prescriptions of the law are to be observed when such permission is granted.

2. No one is to be admitted to the novitiate until he has completed a postulancy of at least two years, or even more if the constitutions so prescribe, under penalty of the invalidity of his subsequent profession.

3. The novitiate is not to be started before the twenty-first year, according to the law now in force, and it is to last one or even two years, according to the constitutions of the respective Order.

4. After the novitiate, with all other prescriptions properly fulfilled, lay religious can be admitted to simple vows. While these vows are taken as perpetual on the part of the religious, their juridical consequences will bind the Order for a period of six years.

5. When six years have been spent in simple vows, and with the completion of the thirtieth year of age, and not before, under penalty of invalidity, only when

all the other prescriptions of the law have been duly observed, lay religious may be admitted to solemn vows.

6. The prescriptions regarding simple and solemn vows as enacted in the preceding articles are to be observed also by lay brothers now living in monasteries, if they have not as yet made their solemn profession.

This long space of nine years, it is hoped, will enable superiors to ascertain the constancy of their subjects, and will give the subjects an opportunity to acquire a thorough knowledge of the life they intend to embrace with solemn vows, so that they can do this after being more firmly grounded in virtue and more richly endowed with a mature judgment.

This should give some hope of later perseverance, but even this hope will not be entirely trustworthy unless there be employed, together with other similar helps, the following precautions and safeguards, which the Holy See has strongly recommended through the centuries, and which the better disciplined religious societies have found successful in practice.

In the first place, the admission of prospective *conversi* is to follow only upon the making of many and diligent inquiries, and the employment of all due cautions. The provincial superior must learn whether the candidate is of legitimate birth, of good morals, of high regard among the people, whether he has the proper docility of a recruit in religion, and especially whether he is moved by the right kind of motive in embracing the religious state. For there are many who seem to enter religion to seek after a soft life rather than to leave it, who seek "in the monastery what they could not afford outside" (*Reg.* S. Aug., c. I, 3),[45] or who want to lead an easy life which is free from cares, unworthy of the honor shown it. . . . These indeed are religious in garb only, and not in virtue, and they would have done better to walk the broad ways of the world than to endanger perhaps their eternal salvation by pretending to things above them.

Only those who have been found worthy after even secret investigations, and who are well recommended in the light of the documents furnished, are to be admitted to the postulancy, with the customary permission of the major superiors.

[45] *MPL,* XXXIII, 960, where the citation occurs in *Epistola CCXI,* n. 5.

"It has been sufficiently demonstrated," says Clement VIII in his instruction for the reception and education of novices, *Cum ad regularem,* §15, "that the perfect education of *conversi* brings honor and glory to the religious state, and gives a useful and edifying example to the faithful." It is necessary therefore that from the very beginning the religious spirit and that of their Order pervade their whole soul. . . .

For this purpose, a father, recommended by the maturity of his years and the manner of his life, is to be placed over the postulants.

A beginning often has to be made by teaching the very rudiments of civility, as candidates for the lay brotherhood often come from among the less privileged. Boorishness in manners and speech, in walking and eating, is to be gradually but in the end thoroughly rooted out. A soiled garb, when it is not worn for the love of humility and the contempt of the world, but rather because of uncouth negligence, does not savor of the spirit of Christ and therefore does not always augur well for the man who wears it. Personal cleanliness and neatness in dress, always with due modesty and simplicity, are to be greatly cultivated. The ordinary rules of politeness which an urbane education postulates for social conduct should be observed also in monasteries, as fraternal charity demands, for the charitable man avoids annoying his neighbors. The rudeness of those who seek only their own pleasure, to the neglect of others, is bound to be irksome to the brethren and to give them plenty of occasion for exercising their patience.

This external discipline will lead to a proper character development, imparting a noble delicacy of spirit which avoids every least offense to others, which anticipates their wishes, and which shows an habitually pleasant disposition, preferring others to self.

It is important, however, that Christian charity vivify, rule and ennoble these various actions, so that whatever is praiseworthy and pleasing to others in our words, deeds and forbearance proceed from a heart filled with charity.

If all these things are befitting in lay religious, all the more must they stand out in the priests, and in the clerics who are destined for the priesthood, so that through the contemplation of the example of those who are above them the *conversi* may be led along the path not only of virtue, but also of courtesy and politeness.

Thus, by instruction, encouragement, patience and especially by example, it will not be hard to raise the manners and habits of the more uncouth to a culture and grace that will soon after their entrance into religion justify the application of these words of St. Bernard to them, "They have clothed themselves with a chastened mien and deportment, they have adorned their bodily bearing with graceful poise and gravity . . . a greater moderation in speech, a happier expression of face, a more modest appearance in company, a more sedate manner of life. . . ." (*Serm.* 63, *in Cant.*, n. 6.)[46]

That the spiritual training may produce these fruits should be the whole ambition of the superior of the postulants and of the master of novices. These directors should make it their pride and duty, . . . to promote the progress of the lay brothers in the way of holiness.

In accord with the decrees of the Holy See, they shall explain all of Christian doctrine, and especially what pertains to the proper and fruitful reception of the sacraments of Penance and Holy Communion, using as their guide the Catechism of the Council of Trent for pastors. At the same time they shall teach them the obligations they will assume at religious profession and the virtues they must cultivate to lead the life of the vows. Likewise they shall explain the parts of the rule and of the constitutions which pertain to the *conversi*.

Conferences or sermons shall be given to the lay brothers on specified days, not only to the juniors but to all, including the seniors in profession and in years. The content-matter in these sermons or conferences shall deal not only with the catechism, with the counsels of the spiritual life, with an explanation of the rule and the constitutions, but also with the practical norms and examples of a modest and composed refinement of manners.

The superiors shall seek to develop in the souls of the lay religious those virtues and safeguards which are especially necessary for their state in life, namely humility, obedience, the spirit of prayer, and the idea of working for a supernatural reward.

And in the first place, the lay brothers should strive for interior and exterior humility. . . .

The *conversi* shall likewise excel in their obedience.

[46] *MPL*, CLXXXIII, 1083.

They must know that in this submission of their will they are safeguarded from the danger of sin; that with obedience they are assured of victory, that with it they will gain an impregnable defence, numberless merits, the highest peace. It is important that this obedience be fortified with supernatural motives. According to the writings of the saints, our superiors are God's representatives placed over us. . . .

The spirit of prayer must also be diligently promoted. "Diligence in prayer is of the first necessity to thee, for prayer is an impenetrable armour, a certain refuge, a secure haven, and a most safe stronghold. . . ." (Louis Blosius, *Canon vitae spirit.*, c. 17, n. 1.)[47] Clement VIII likewise prescribed for the religious instruction of *conversi:* "They shall be diligently taught, according to their capacity and opportunity, concerning spiritual doctrine, especially concerning the manner of engaging in mental prayer." (*Instr. super rec. et educ. Novit.*, n. 22.)[48]

Care must therefore be taken that the lay brothers know well the virtue and the exercise of prayer; that at the appointed hours they give themselves faithfully to vocal and mental prayer; that for the full time prescribed in the constitutions of their Order they devote themselves to prayer alone. It is not enough for them to make their meditation while they are serving Mass. The superiors are to watch, especially after the lay brothers have finished their novitiate, that these will make their meditations and say their prayers.

The lay brothers shall make constant use throughout the day of the short prayers known as ejaculations. For this is a direct way to assure the soul's union with God, to gain an increase of merit, to keep a right intention, to forestall and overcome temptations, to sanctify their whole life.

They shall likewise make a holy thing of their manual labor, which is the chief work of the lay brothers in monasteries, not serving to the eye nor working for human praise, but seeking only the will of God and their superiors. . . .

---

[47] The English version given here is from the anonymous translation revised and edited by Delany, *The Paradise of the Faithful Soul, Part I—A Rule of the Spiritual Life (Canon Vitae Spiritualis)* (London: Burns, Oates and Washbourne, Ltd., 1926), p. 59.

[48] *Cum ad regularem,* 19 mart. 1603, §15—*Fontes,* n. 189.

To accomplish all these things the lay brothers shall approach the altar table for frequent and even daily Holy Communion, according to the rules in recent instructions of the Holy See. Likewise they are to have a very special devotion to the Blessed Virgin Mother of God, whom they shall always call upon, honor and imitate as their most dear mother.

The superiors shall also see to it that the priests and lay brothers practice the utmost mutual courtesy and charity. The *conversi* shall reverence the priests, who minister to them and deliver to them the most sacred mysteries. The priests shall honor the lay brothers and "strive . . . to take pride in associating with the brothers who have dedicated their lives to poverty." (St. Augustine, *Reg.*, c. I, 5.)[49] Priests are to remember that many lay religious have after their death been canonized as saints and numbered among the blessed for the devotion with which they worked at the humbler tasks throughout their lives. They shall therefore have a loving respect for the mode of life led by the lay brothers, since it has furnished an approach to such many-sided and wondrous holiness.

Lest the exercise of important offices in the monastery cause the lay brothers to grow proud, and being puffed up to look down upon the priests, the higher offices of this kind shall not be assigned to them, unless it is absolutely necessary. Whatever assignment is given shall be entrusted only in complete dependence on and obedience to a senior and wise superior, to whom they are to give a faithful account of what they do and plan.

Let these few admonitions culled out from among many suffice.

For the rest, this Sacred Congregation is most confident that the superiors general of all the religious Orders will strive with all their might to promote this kind of life for their lay brothers. Let their forbearance be so tempered with vigilance that discipline too will remain on guard. . . .

All these presents having been brought before His Holiness Pope Pius X, he has deigned to approve and ratify them, everything to the contrary notwithstanding, even though it be deserving of special mention.

---

[49] *MPL,* XXXIII, 960, where the citation occurs in *Epistola CCXI,* n. 6.

## PART TWO

## CANONICAL COMMENTARY

# CHAPTER IV

# THE STATUS OF *CONVERSI* SINCE THE CODE

The present Code of Canon Law, promulgated on May 27, 1917, and in force since May 19, 1918,[1] made no change in the traditional legal status of *conversi* professed with solemn vows. As before, when both *conversi*[2] and *conversae*[3] received full recognition as religious, so in the Code they are acknowledged as belonging to the religious state.[4]

*Conversi* professed with simple vows, however, were officially raised to the status of true religious for the first time with the promulgation of the Code. The new definition of "religious" in canon 488, 7°, includes those who are professed with simple vows, whereas they were formerly not admitted to be such.[5] History repeated itself, therefore, when *conversi* who canonically were not religious were raised to that status in the twentieth

[1] Benedictus XV, const. *Providentissima Mater Ecclesia,* 27 maii 1917—*Codex Iuris Canonici Pii X Pontificis Maximi iussu digestus Benedicti Papae XV auctoritate promulgatus* (ed. Gasparri, Romae: Typis Polyglottis Vaticanis, 1917. Reimpressio, 1934), pp. xlv–xlix.

[2] C. 7, X, *de regularibus et transeuntibus ad religionem,* III, 31; Benedictus XIV, decr. 21 mart. 1747—Bizzarri, *Coll. S. C. Ep. et Reg.,* pp. 407–409.

[3] S. C. Ep. et Reg., *Gratianopolitana Conversarum,* iul. 1703—Bizzarri, *Coll. S. C. Ep. et Reg.,* p. 318.

[4] Cans. 488, 7°; 539, §1; 564; 565; 610, §3.

[5] Benedictus XIV, const. *Quamvis iusto,* 30 apr. 1749—*Fontes,* n. 398; S. C. Ep. et Reg., *Cenomanen.,* 19 apr. 1844—*Fontes,* n. 1938; S. C. super Statu Regularium, litt. encycl. *Neminem latet,* 19 mart. 1857—*Fontes,* n. 4381; S. C. Ep. et Reg., *Congregationis Presbyterorum Saecularium,* 16 sept 1864—*Fontes,* n. 1993.

century by the promulgation of the Code, just as in the eleventh century the servant *conversi* were first made religious by the *Constitutiones Hirsaugienses.*[6]

This was no sudden innovation, however, since the Roman Curia had already begun under Pope Leo XIII (1878–1903) to extend the name "religious" to those who were professed with simple vows, first by virtue of indult and then by common law.[7]

The Code's law for *conversi* is the same for those who are professed with simple as for those who are professed with solemn vows, except in matters directly consequent on the concept of solemnity in the profession, namely, the invalidity of the subsequent marriage and the complete inhibition of the right of proprietorship.[8]

## §1. "Conversi" and the Religious State

*Religious* are those who make profession in an ecclesiastically approved society whose members, in following the laws proper to their institute, take public vows, either perpetual or temporary—the latter being subject to renewal when they have expired—and thus strive to gain evangelical perfection.[9] When *conversi* take their vows as here prescribed they are recognized as members of the religious state. Thus there is vindicated for them the right to that honor which is due to religious. Regarding this canon 487 prescribes:

> The religious state, or the permanent common life in which the faithful undertake by means of the vows of obedience, chastity and poverty, to observe the evan-

[6] S. Wilhelmi *Constitutiones Hirsaugienses,* lib. 1, c. 38; lib. 2, c. 11—Herrgott, *Vetus Disciplina Monastica,* pp. 413, 485.

[7] Molitor, *Capita Selecta,* pp. 135, 173; Oesterle, *Praelectiones,* I, 239; Schaefer, *De Religiosis,* n. 46, 5, a.

[8] Cans. 579; 580; 1119; 1308, §2.

[9] Can. 488: "In canonibus qui sequuntur, veniunt nomine:

"1°. *Religionis,* societas, a legitima ecclesiastica auctoritate approbata, in qua sodales, secundum proprias ipsius societatis leges, vota publica, perpetua vel temporaria, elapso tamen tempore renovanda, nuncupant, atque ita ad evangelicam perfectionem tendunt; . . .

"7°. *Religiosorum,* qui vota nuncuparunt in aliqua religione; . . ."

gelical counsels in addition to the ordinary commandments is to be held in honor by all.[10]

In what manner religious are to be "held in honor" is partly specified in other canons of the Code, but this common duty receives its closer interpretation mainly in the letters of the Popes and in the instructions of the Sacred Congregations, which documents in large part simply vindicate for religious their claim in equity to the special honor and reverence due them from all the faithful.

Canon 491, §1, states that "religious hold precedence over lay people; clerical religious institutes over lay institutes; canons regular over monks; monks over other regulars; regulars over members of religious congregations; pontifical congregations over diocesan congregations; . . ."[11] *Conversi,* therefore, must be given a place of honor higher than that of the laity. Further, when their institute appears in a body in public, they are not to be separated from their clerical confrères, and thus will obtain precedence even over priests if these belong to institutes classified in a lower rank by this canon.[12]

The principal rights vindicated for religious, and therefore for *conversi,* by the express provision of the Code are the privileges of clerics mentioned in canons 119 to 123, and extended to religious by the provision of canon 614. Religious are not free to renounce these privileges any more than clerics, according to canon 123.[13] Canon 592 makes the corresponding obligations of clerics, as enumerated in canons 124 to 142, except those which are precluded by the context of the law or by the nature of the matter, binding upon all religious.

---

[10] "Status religiosus seu stabilis in communi vivendi modus, quo fideles, praeter communia praecepta, evangelica quoque consilia servanda per vota obedientiae, castitatis et paupertatis suscipiunt, ab omnibus in honore habendus est."

[11] "Religiosi praecedunt laicis; religiones clericales, laicalibus; canonici regulares, monachis; monachi, ceteris regularibus; regulares, Congregationibus religiosis; Congregationes iuris pontificii, Congregationibus iuris dioecesani; . . ."

[12] Schaefer, *De Religiosis,* n. 57.

[13] *Op. cit.,* n. 390, 1.

Pope Pius XI (1922–1939) gave the following exhortation to all superiors of religious communities of men in his Apostolic Letter *Unigenitus* on March 19, 1924:[14]

> We shall now consider those religious who, although they are not called to the priesthood, nevertheless take the same religious vows as priests, and are therefore no less bound before God and held to the duty of striving after perfection. . . . We can not refrain here, dearly beloved sons, from exhorting you to reflect on what a grave duty you have of watching that the *conversi,* both during their novitiate and throughout their lives, be furnished with the spiritual helps they need to go forward and persevere, these helps being perhaps the greater in proportion to the lowliness of their status and the humble work they have to do. For this reason, superiors, in deciding where each one of them is to be stationed and what work he is to do, must consider each individual's talents, and the obstacles that may perhaps confront him. And if the *conversi* ever fall off in their religious fervor, the superiors shall leave no stone unturned in their fatherly solicitude, to lead them back gently but firmly to holiness of life. But most of all the superiors are not to neglect the instruction of the lay brothers, either personally or through priests who are properly qualified, in the eternal and sublime truths of the faith, which if known and frequently called to mind furnish many incentives to virtue for any man, whether living in the world or within monastery walls. We wish these things which we have just said to be applied also to all the members of lay congregations, for it is especially necessary that these receive a higher instruction in religion, which goes beyond what is ordinarily taught the faithful, inasmuch as these religious frequently devote themselves to the education of children and adolescents.

The *conversi* must realize that they have joined the monastery not to make a name for themselves by their skill in a secular profession, but rather to embrace a life of prayer and to work for God's glory, their own salvation, and the good of their order:[15]

---

[14] *AAS,* XVI (1924), 146-147.

[15] S. C. de Religiosis, decr. *Sacrosancta,* 1 ian. 1911—*Fontes,* n. 4407.

> They shall likewise make a holy thing of their manual labor, which is the chief work of the lay brothers in monasteries, not serving to the eye nor working for human praise, but seeking only the will of God and their superiors. . . .
>
> Lest the exercise of important offices in the monastery cause the lay brothers to grow proud, and being puffed up to look down upon the priests, the higher offices of this kind shall not be assigned to them, unless it is absolutely necessary. Whatever assignment is given shall be entrusted only in complete dependence on and obedience to a senior and wise superior, to whom they are to give a faithful account of what they do and plan. . . .

The faithful living outside of monasteries are also bound by the prescription of canon 487 which insists that "the religious state . . . is to be held in honor by all." This acknowledgment of honor postulates a proper appreciation of supernatural values, the lack of which Pope Leo XIII deprecated in his Letter *Testem benevolentiae,* directed to Cardinal Gibbons: [16]

> . . . Certainly the help of the Holy Spirit is absolutely necessary for cultivating the virtues: but these innovators place too much importance on the *natural virtues,* as if these were better adapted to the needs and customs of our days . . . It is difficult indeed to understand how people imbued with Christian wisdom can prefer the natural virtues to the supernatural, and attribute greater efficacy and fruitfulness to them. . . .
>
> A natural consequence of this near-contempt for the evangelical virtues, which they falsely call passive, has been the dissemination of a low regard for the religious life as well. . . . But the falsity of their assertions is easily seen from the doctrine and practice of the Church, which has always approved the religious life very highly. . . .

There is certainly a widespread lack of proper appreciation among the faithful for the religious vocation as such, and consequently also for the lay brotherhood which is devoted to the discharge of manual labor. Father William Schaefers, who has

[16] 22 ian. 1899—*ASS,* XXXI (1898–1899), 475, 477.

studied the problems of lay brothers in the United States and has written several articles on the subject, notes:

> Monastic authorities nearly all lament the fact that so few, comparatively speaking, are interested in and concerned with fostering vocations of this kind. This lack of interest and concern prevails everywhere, even among priests and Sisters. There are thousands of young Catholic men who have no idea of what the religious lay life is, no idea of the perfection of the Brother's vocation, and for want of instruction this ignorance continues. . . .[17]
>
> Supernaturally speaking, the brother vocation is a very, very high one. But the world today is openly antagonistic toward it. Parents do not favor it, neither do priests. The lowliness of the vocation is a great hindrance, socially speaking. According to worldly standards—that more or less influence all of us—the boy who aspires to become a brother aspires to very little. . . .[18]

## §2. Relations of "Conversi" to Clerics and Other Religious

Book II of the Code of Canon Law, which contains the legislation for persons in the Church, is divided for practical reasons [19] into three parts, the first being devoted to clerics, the second to religious, and the third to the laity. Whereas the faithful in the first and third groups belong to separate and mutually exclusive categories "by divine institution," [20] those of the intermediate

[17] "The Brother Problem,"—*The Homiletic and Pastoral Review* (New York: Joseph F. Wagner, Inc., 1900–), XXXII (1931–1932), 386. This article appeared in two installments in the *Review,* XXXII (1931–1932), 61–67 and 381–386.

[18] "A Preparatory School for Brothers,"—*The Ecclesiastical Review* (Philadelphia: The American Ecclesiastical Review, 1889–1943; Washington, D. C.: The Catholic University of America, 1944–), CIII (1940), 72. Cf. Garesché, "What Should Priests Think of the Brother's Vocation?"—*ER,* LXXIX (1928), 269–285. The St. John Bosco Vocation Club should help remedy this situation. Cf. Ohligslager, "A New Approach in the Field of Vocations,"—*ER,* CIV (1941), 356–358.

[19] Larraona, "Commentarium,"—*CpR,* I (1920), 16–21.

[20] Can. 107. Cf. Champoux, "The Clerical and Lay State versus the Re-

group, the religious, are necessarily at the same time members of either the first or the third class, in accord with the fact that they are clerics or non-clerics. When canon 487 speaks of the religious state as connoting an established and fixed manner of life, and prescribes that it is to be held in honor by all, it does not imply that the non-clerical members of that state are raised by some sort of quasi-ordination above their hierarchical status of lay folk. Canon 107 says explicitly that there are "lay religious" in the Catholic Church:

> By divine institution there are in the Church *clerics* distinct from the *lay folk,* although not all clerics belong to a rank which is of divine foundation. Members of either group may be *religious.*[21]

Canon 1342, §2, says the same: "All lay men, including religious, are forbidden to preach in church."[22] It is to this category of lay religious that the *conversi* belong, inasmuch as they are not clerics.

The term "*conversus*" is not defined in the Code. Canon 488, which furnishes the technical terminology for the law for religious, defines (n. 7°) "*religious*" as persons "who take vows in a religious institute." It goes on to distinguish and define the various kinds of religious: "*Religious professed with simple vows* [are those] who take vows in a religious Congregation; *regulars,* who take vows in an Order; *sisters,* women religious professed with simple vows; *nuns,* women religious professed with solemn vows or, unless the nature of the case or the context demand otherwise, women religious whose institute has a right to call for a profession with solemn vows, but in some places by command of the Holy See actually calls for a profession with only simple vows; . . ."[23]

ligious State,"—*The Jurist* (Washington, D. C.: The School of Canon Law, The Catholic University of America, 1941–), I (1941), 135–138.

[21] "Ex divina institutione sunt in Ecclesia *clerici* a *laicis* distincti, licet non omnes clerici sint divinae institutionis; utrique autem possunt esse *religiosi.*"

[22] "Concionari in ecclesia vetantur laici omnes, etsi religiosi."

[23] Can. 488: "In canonibus qui sequuntur, veniunt nomine: . . .

"7°. *Religiosorum,* qui vota nuncuparunt in aliqua religione; *religiosorum*

The term "*conversus*" may be defined as designating a second, non-clerical or non-monastic group of religious devoted *ex professo* to manual labor in clerical or monastic communities admitting this additional class.[24] An application of the definitions of canon 488 cited in the paragraph *supra* shows that *conversi* who take vows in an order are acknowledged by the Code as being "regulars." Women religious who are *conversae* are further designated as "sisters" if they are professed with simple vows, or as "nuns" if they are professed with solemn vows.[25]

The Code plainly implies that the *conversi* may take solemn vows.[26]

The word "monk" is another term designating a class of religious, which, like the name "*conversus*," is not defined in the Code. Those who understand the term "monk" as applicable to all religious who take vows in an institute following a monastic rule logically regard the *conversi* as a species of monks.[27] A comparison of the use of the terms "monk" and "*conversus*" since the time of Blessed William of Hirsau (+ 1091),[28] and especially after Pope Callistus II approved the Cistercian *Exordium parvum* in 1119,[29] however, shows that the two words are rather to be understood as the technical designations for two

---

*votorum simplicium,* qui in Congregatione religiosa; *regularium,* qui in Ordine; *sororum,* religiosae votorum simplicium; *monialium,* religiosae votorum sollemnium aut, nisi ex rei natura vel ex contextu sermonis aliud constet, religiosae quarum vota ex instituto sunt sollemnia, sed pro aliquibus locis ex Apostolicae Sedis praescripto sunt simplicia; . . ."

[24] Oesterle, *Praelectiones,* I, 283. Cf. also *supra,* pp. 20, 22, 25-26.

[25] Cf. *AAS,* XXXIII (1941), 168-169. Extern sisters, who today do the work of the original *conversi,* are limited to profession with simple vows. —S. C. de Religiosis, decr. 16 iul. 1931—Bouscaren, *The Canon Law Digest,* II (Milwaukee: Bruce, 1943), 171. But the limitation applies only to externs, and not to the *conversae,* who keep perpetual cloister along with the choir nuns.

[26] Can. 610, §3: "In eisdem religionibus sive virorum sive mulierum [quibus est chori obligatio], sollemniter professi qui a choro abfuerunt, debent, exceptis conversis, horas canonicas privatim recitare."

[27] Thus Delatte-McCann, *Commentary on the Rule of St. Benedict* (London, 1921), p. 366.

[28] Cf. *supra,* p. 15.

[29] Cf. *supra,* pp. 17, 20-23, 25.

mutually exclusive groups of religious living side by side in monastic communities. This distinction of "*conversi*" from "monks" is acknowledged in canonical legislation.[30] Any closer specification of the connotation of these terms as used in a particular institute must be sought in the constitutions of the order or congregation itself.

"Monks" can prove from history that they are the direct descendants of the first followers of the ancient monastic rules, and that the *conversi* institute is an innovation originating in the Benedictine order and dating only from the eleventh century. The original reasons for the monks' higher domestic rank as religious, besides their being first in the order of time, were their professed pursuance of the contemplative life and their public celebration of the divine office in choir.[31] But for many centuries the monks have differed from their ancient spiritual fathers in that they became a clerical body, whereas the ancient monks were generally non-clerical. Herein lies a new reason for the preference and precedence of choir monks over *conversi*. It is because the former are a clerical body and belong to that class of Catholics who by divine institution are placed over the rest of the faithful to rule and sanctify them.[32]

In the case of women religious the original reason for the distinction between choir and lay nuns obtains, namely, the former group's dedication to the contemplative life and its obligation of reciting the divine office.[33] Choir nuns can not belong to the clerical state in any way,[34] so the modern, added reason for the distinction between choir monks and *conversi* in orders of men does not apply in the case of women religious.

The strictly ecclesiastical jurisdiction which clerical religious

---

[30] Benedictus XIV, decr. 21 mart. 1747—Bizzarri, *Coll. S. C. Ep. et Reg.*, pp. 407–409.

[31] Cf. can. 491, §1; St. Thomas, *Summa Theologica* (6 vols., Taurini: Marietti, 1938), II–II, q. CLXXXVIII, a. 6.

[32] Cans. 107, 118, 948. Cf. Wernz, *Ius Decretalium*, III (2. ed., Romae, 1908), n. 682.

[33] Cf. can. 610, §§1, 3.

[34] Can. 968, §1, says only a baptized *man* (*vir*) can validly receive holy Orders.

institutes exercise in virtue of the privilege of exemption[35] is perhaps the strongest reason for the exclusion of their lay members from chapter rights.[36] At the same time it seems only fair that the professed *conversi* be at least informally consulted in an institute whose constitutions provide that the superior and the clerical chapter admit brother novices to vows. The reasons for asking their opinion are that they will have to accept the recruits as their confrères, and live and work with them; and that their judgment regarding their fitness for this manner of religious life is not to be despised.[37]

*Conversi* are not particularly benefited when their constitutions[38] admit to their institutes so-called "religious" oblates, "who in all things are to be considered as lay brothers," but who are not religious at all, inasmuch as they have not taken any vows.

A certain separation between the various classes in religious communities is necessary for the sake of forestalling and obviating the very real scandal that can be engendered by mutual jealousy. If non-clerical religious are not restrained in their possible interassociation with the clerical religious it is likely that they may become envious of the greater latitude of movement on the part of the priests of the community, inasmuch as the latter may repeatedly be called on to go outside their monasteries for discharging the work of the pastoral ministry. In like manner the clerical members of the community, feeling themselves burdened with studies and cares, may become prone to compare their own lot with that of the *conversi*, and thereupon to sense a conviction that the latter have duties of too light a character to permit them to carry their share of the community's

---

[35] Can. 501, §1.

[36] Cf. c. 32, *de electione et electi potestate*, I, 6, in VI°; Wernz, *op. cit.*, III, n. 685; Schaefer, *De Religiosis*, n. 128, 4; Augustine, *A Commentary on the New Code of Canon Law* (8 vols., Vol. III; 5. ed., St. Louis: Herder, 1938), III, 109. To be cited as *Commentary.*

[37] *Report of the Benedictine Brother Instructors' Convention, 1942*, pp. 139–141.

[38] Cf. *Declarationes in Sacram Regulam et Constitutiones Congregationis Helveto-Americanae O.S.B.*, n. 91.

work. The relations between clerical and lay religious should be founded on the right predicated in canon 682:

> The laity have the right to receive from the clergy, in accord with the Church's disciplinary legislation, the benefit of the Church's spiritual goods, and especially the helps necessary for salvation.[39]

### §3. Qualifications Required in "Conversi" Candidates

The general qualifications necessary for a person to be admitted into a monastery as a *conversus* are the same as those which are required for the admission of any religious. Canon 538 reads:

> Any Catholic who is not prevented by a legal impediment, and who has a right intention and is able to carry the burdens of the religious life, may be admitted into religion.[40]

The first and basic qualification which the Code requires of an aspirant to the religious life is membership in the Catholic faith, for the religious state is by very definition[41] an established and fixed mode of life within the Church, wherein certain members of the faithful undertake to live the Christian life in its full perfection. Juridically there can be no perfection of the Christian life except in a member of the Church who is in good standing; it is useless to pretend to an observance of the counsels if the precepts are neglected.[42]

Secondly, the candidate for the religious life, and therefore the prospective *conversus,* must not be "prevented by a legal impediment." The legal impediment of deficiency in years is enacted in canons 555, §1, 1°; 572 and 573: fifteen completed years of life are postulated for admission into the novitiate,

---

[39] "Laici ius habent recipiendi a clero, ad normam ecclesiasticae disciplinae, spiritualia bona et potissimum adiumenta ad salutem necessaria."

[40] "In religionem admitti potest quilibet catholicus qui nullo legitimo detineatur impedimento rectaque intentione moveatur, et ad religionis onera ferenda sit idoneus."

[41] Can. 487.

[42] Augustine, *Commentary,* III, 198.

sixteen for the making of one's temporary profession, and twenty-one for the making of one's perpetual profession, whether solemn or simple. The higher ages required on the part of *conversi* by the decree *Sacrosancta* on January 1, 1911, were abrogated by the Code, according to canon 6, 1° and 6°, although they may still be required by the constitutions of a particular religious institute.[43] Since no specified age is demanded for entering the postulancy, *conversi* aspirants can, according to the letter of the law, be admitted at any time, but those who have not as yet attained the age of puberty need the permission of their parents.[44] Such boys or girls should not begin their postulancy, which immediately precedes the novitiate, before they are fourteen years and six months old, or at least fourteen years, according to canon 539, §§1 and 2, which prescribes a postulancy of six months, or of not more than a year at the discretion of the major superior, for *conversi* in institutes of perpetual vows. If the constitutions prescribe or permit a longer postulancy, the age at which it may be begun can be correspondingly lowered.[45]

The other legal impediments to admission in the novitiate are enumerated in canon 542: "They are admitted . . . invalidly: who have belonged to a non-Catholic sect; . . . who enter the religious institute through force, grave fear or fraud, or whom the religious superior receives, being himself influenced in any of these ways; a married person, as long as obliged by the bond of matrimony; persons who are bound or who have in the past been bound by the tie of religious profession; those who are subject to punishment for a grave crime committed, of which they have been accused or can be accused; a bishop whether residential or titular, although he has only been named by the Roman Pontiff; clerics who by provision of the Holy See are bound by oath to give their services for the work of their diocese or

---

[43] S. C. de Religiosis, 6 oct. 1919—*AAS,* XI (1919), 420; "Annotationes,"—*CpR,* I (1920), 354–356.

[44] Schaefer, *De Religiosis,* n. 213, 1, b. Can. 88, §2, states that puberty is to be reckoned as attained by boys at the completion of their fourteenth year, by girls at the completion of their twelfth.

[45] Cf. Oesterle, *Praelectiones,* I, 284; Creusen-Garesché-Ellis, *Religious Men and Women in the Code* (4. ed., Milwaukee: Bruce, 1942), n. 172.

missions, for as long a time as the obligation of the oath shall last. Illicitly but validly are admitted: clerics in sacred Orders if they have not consulted the local ordinary, or if the latter has refused permission inasmuch as their departure would occasion grave loss to souls, which could not be averted in any other way; those who have debts they cannot pay; those who are subject to rendering account or involved in other secular business regarding which the religious institute might fear lawsuits and difficulties; children who are bound to help their parents, that is, their father or mother, grandfather or grandmother, who are in grave need; and parents whose help is necessary to support or educate their children; . . . Orientals in religious institutes of the Latin discipline without the written permission of the Sacred Congregation for the Oriental Church."[46]

[46] Can. 542: "Firmo praescripto can. 539–541, aliisque in propriis cuiusque religionis constitutionibus,

"1°. Invalide ad novitiatum admittuntur:

"Qui sectae acatholicae adhaeserunt;

"Qui aetatem ad novitiatum requisitam non habent;

"Qui religionem ingrediuntur vi, metu gravi aut dolo inducti, vel quos Superior eodem modo inductus recipit;

"Coniux, durante matrimonio;

"Qui obstringuntur vel obstricti fuerunt vinculo professionis religiosae;

"Hi quibus imminet poena ob grave delictum commissum de quo accusati sunt vel accusari possunt;

"Episcopus sive residentialis sive titularis licet a Romano Pontifice sit tantum designatus;

"Clerici qui ex instituto Sanctae Sedis iureiurando tenentur operam suam navare in bonum suae dioecesis vel missionum, pro eo tempore quo iurisiurandi obligatio perdurat.

"2°. Illicite, sed valide admittuntur:

"Clerici in sacris constituti, inconsulto loci Ordinario aut eodem contradicente ex eo quod eorum discessus in grave animarum detrimentum cedat, quod aliter vitari minime possit;

"Aero alieno gravati qui solvendo pares non sint;

"Reddendae rationi obnoxii aut aliis saecularibus negotiis implicati, ex quibus lites et molestias religio timere possit;

"Filii qui parentibus, idest patri vel matri, avo vel aviae, in gravi necessitate constitutis, opitulari debent, et parentes quorum opera sit ad liberos alendos vel educandos necessaria;

"Ad sacerdotium in religione destinati, a quo tamen removeantur irregularitate aliove canonico impedimento;

The other legal impediments to admission to the making of one's profession are enumerated in canon 572: "For the validity of every religious profession it is required that: . . . the lawful superior named in the constitutions admits to profession the subject desiring to take vows; a valid novitiate according to the norm of canon 555 have been completed; the profession be made without force, grave fear or fraud; that it be express; that it be received by the lawful superior named in the constitutions either personally or through a delegate. For the validity, however, of a perpetual profession, whether solemn or simple, it is further required that it have been preceded by a simple temporary profession according to the norm of canon 574." [47]

The third requisite for the candidate who aspires to the religious brotherhood is a proper motive. His reason for joining the monastery must be to serve God, or to save his soul, or to work for the good of the Church or of the religious institute, for:

> All . . . religious . . . are bound not only to keep their vows faithfully, but also to mold their lives according to the rules and constitutions of their respective institutes, and thus to strive for the perfection of their state.[48]

---

"Orientales in latinis religionibus sine venia scripto data Sacrae Congregationis pro Ecclesia Orientali."

[47] Can. 572: "§1. Ad validitatem cuiusvis religiosae professionis requiritur ut:

"1°. Qui eam emissurus est, legitimam aetatem habeat ad normam can. 573;

"2°. Eum ad professionem admittat legitimus Superior secundum constitutiones;

"3°. Novitiatus validus ad normam can. 555 praecesserit;

"4°. Professio sine vi aut metu gravi aut dolo emittatur;

"5°. Sit expressa;

"6°. A legitimo Superiore secundum constitutiones per se vel per alium recipiatur.

"§2. Ad validitatem vero professionis perpetuae sive sollemnis sive simplicis, requiritur insuper ut praecesserit professio simplex temporaria ad normam can. 574."

[48] Can. 593: "Omnes . . . religiosi . . . debent, non solum quae nuncuparunt vota fideliter integreque servare, sed etiam secundum regulas et constitutiones propriae religionis vitam componere atque ita ad perfectionem sui status contendere."

Pope Clement VIII's Constitution *Cum ad regularem* obliged religious superiors to investigate into the aspirants' motives:

> The superiors shall search out diligently what spirit, intention and desire leads them to choose the regular life, what was their purpose in coming—whether it was an ambition for virtue and a more perfect life, to be more free to serve God, or whether it was levity, human affection, or a downright mistake . . .[49]

Lastly the candidate must be "able to carry the burdens of the religious life," and, specifically, of that form of the religious life which he has chosen. For *conversi,* according to many religious constitutions which follow the Cistercian *Regula conversorum,* this specific requirement is the ability to do manual labor.

On the other hand, the aspirant to the lay brotherhood need not have the qualifications, least of all the aptitude for higher studies, required in a man who wants to become a priest. In fact, clerical religious and those who aspire to this state may be given the option, in case they find they are unable to make the required studies, of transferring to the class of *conversi.*[50]

The documents necessary for all candidates for the religious life are baptismal and confirmation certificates.[51] Men or boys need also testimonial letters from the local ordinaries of their place of origin and of every other diocese or territory wherein they lived for more than a morally continuous year after they became fourteen years of age.[52] All aspirants to the religious life who have been in a seminary or a college which exists for the purpose of imparting a religious or clerical training, or in the postulancy or novitiate of another religious institute, need also testimonial letters from the rector of the school or from the major religious superior.[53] Women and girls are not to be re-

[49] 19 mart. 1603, §5—*Fontes,* n. 189.

[50] Goyeneche, "Consultationes,"—*CpR,* III (1922), 10–13, 82–84.

[51] Can. 544, §1.

[52] Can. 544, §2. The obligation of the superiors to obtain these and the other testimonial letters required by can. 544 is a grave one. A special sanction is invoked by the penal law enacted in can. 2411.

[53] Can. 544, §3. Cf. Schaefer, *De Religiosis,* n. 225, c. The joint decree of the Sacred Congregation for Religious and of the Sacred Congregation

ceived without a previous careful investigation of their character and conduct. Finally, the superiors who receive them may require any or all applicants to furnish whatever other documents may seem necessary or useful.[54]

Prospective *conversae* fall under the general laws for women religious regarding the furnishing of the dowry and the investigation of the aspirants' freedom of choice in embracing the convent life.[55]

---

of Seminaries and Universities, issued on July 25, 1941 [*AAS,* XXXIII (1941), 371], which prescribes in its second part that if a candidate for a religious community has left a seminary for any cause at all, the religious superior has to have recourse to the Sacred Congregation for Religious before the candidate can be admitted, is not to be extended to those who aspire to become *conversi.* The wording of the decree does not make this exception and would indeed seem to include prospective *conversi,* but its whole tenor and context insinuate rather candidates for the clerical state. Cf. Frison, "Ex-seminarian and Novice: A Classification,"—*The Jurist,* VI (1946), 417, n. 7. Also *infra.,* p. 73.

[54] Can. 544, §§6, 7.

[55] Cans. 547–552.

# CHAPTER V

## THE SEPARATION OF *CONVERSI* AND THE TRANSFER BETWEEN CLASSES

The Code says very little explicitly regarding the separation of *conversi* and the maintenance of the class distinction between them and other religious, but it constitutes a definite and adequate barrier between these groups by reason of the legislation contained in canon 558. There it is enacted that, when a novitiate is made with a view to becoming a religious in one group or class, such a novitiate will be without valid effect in relation to the other group or class. The fact that a valid novitiate is the indispensable condition for admittance into the religious life [1] makes this a key canon in the whole law for religious, inasmuch as it protects the individuality of the various specific forms of religious life by requiring a different training in preparation for each of them. It also guarantees the stability of the *conversi* institute by providing a sufficient hindrance for lay brothers who might aspire to the clerical state, and for clerics who might want to become lay brothers.

### §1. The Separate Novitiate

Canon 558 prescribes:

> In religious institutes whose members are divided into two classes the novitiate made for a person's incorporation in one such group is not good for his prospective membership in the other group.[2]

A religious institute, therefore, which divides its members into two classes must train its recruits from the very beginning for

[1] Can. 572, §1, 3°.

[2] "In religionibus in quibus duae sunt sodalium classes, novitiatus pro altera classe peractus, pro altera non valet."

one vocation or the other,[3] and vows made for membership in a group different from that for which the novitiate served as a time of probation are invalid.[4] Canon 558 speaks only of institutes whose members belong to two classes, but its rule is to be extended also to communities having more than two classes,[5] since the reasons for the law are the same, namely the maintenance of the separate identity of the several groups and the guarantee of a specific training of the recruits for membership in each of them. The novitiate made in relation to any one of these classes, therefore, would not be good in relation to any of the others.

Vermeersch noted:

> Even if the same training is given to both classes, the very anticipation of one future state in preference to another has a decisive influence on the spirit that pervades the time of probation.[6]

If a religious wanted to transfer to another group, he would be bound in this instance to repeat his novitiate.

Vermeersch continued:

> If however the approved constitutions should provide that only at the end of the novitiate made by all in

---

[3] Oesterle, *Praelectiones,* I, 308. Cf. S. C. de Religiosis, instr. 1 dec. 1931, n. 6: ". . . The ordinary signs of a religious vocation are certainly not sufficient at all in candidates aspiring to the priesthood, but special additional indications pointing to a fitness for the clerical state are required. For this reason the sacred canons prescribe separate novitiates for clerics and for lay brothers, so that the novitiate made with relation to one group is not valid with relation to the other."—*AAS,* XXIV (1932), 76.

[4] Blat, *Commentarium Textus Codicis Iuris Canonici* (5 vols. in 6, Vol. II, 2. ed., Romae, 1921), II, n. 627. To be cited as *Commentarium.*

[5] S. C. de Religiosis, *Statuta a Sororibus Externis Monasteriorum Monialium Cuiusque Ordinis Servanda,* 16 iul. 1931, n. 28—Schaefer, *De Religiosis,* n. 658; also in *Archiv für katholisches Kirchenrecht,* CXIII (1933), 446 sq. This document is not contained in the *AAS.* Cf. Bouscaren, *The Canon Law Digest,* II, 171, for references to literature regarding these *Statuta.*

[6] Vermeersch-Creusen, *Epitome Iuris Canonici* (3 vols., Vol. I, 6. ed., Mechliniae-Romae: Dessain, 1937), I, n. 710. To be cited as *Epitome.*

> common the class to which each should belong be determined, or that some could be admitted as unspecified as to class, the latter to be designated later according to the aptitude they show—neither of these cases falls under the rule of canon 558, which speaks of the novitiate being made for one class or the other . . .[7]

Creusen adds:

> Sometimes the division into two classes does not exist in the constitutions; this is the case, for example, with the Brothers of the Christian Schools, with the Sisters of Notre Dame de Namur, etc. It is foreseen nevertheless, even from the very time of the novitiate, that certain subjects cannot be given any occupations except those which are usually reserved for the lay brothers or the lay sisters. This practical division does not require two different novitiates.[8]

An application of the principle of canon 558 is found in canon 564, §2:

> A separate place is to be assigned to the *conversi* novices.[9]

This §2 of the canon must be compared with §1 for a full understanding of its implications:

> §1. As far as possible the novitiate is to be cut off from that part of the house where the professed live, so that, except for a special reason and with the permission of the superior or the novice master, the novices may have no communication with the professed religious, nor these latter with the novices.[10]

---

[7] *Loc. cit.;* Schaefer, *De Religiosis,* n. 243, 10; Oesterle, *Praelectiones,* I, 308. Since such constitutions contravene the rule of canon 558, one would haye to assume that they were approved since the enactment of the Code.

[8] Creusen-Garesché-Ellis, *Religious Men and Women in the Code,* n. 203. Cf. Schaefer, *De Religiosis,* n. 52.

[9] "Conversis autem novitiis locus separatus adsignetur."

[10] "Novitiatus ab ea parte domus, in qua degunt professi, sit, quantum fieri potest, segregatus ita ut, sine speciali causa ac Superioris vel Magistri licentia, novitii nullam habeant communicationem cum professis, neque hi cum novitiis."

Like canon 558, canon 564 is taken substantially from Pope Clement VIII's Constitution *Cum ad regularem,* which document is the source most frequently cited in Gasparri's footnotes to the Code's article " On the Training of Novices." [11] It is noteworthy also that most of the Code's legislation for *conversi* is taken from that of Clement VIII, and his *Cum ad regularem* provides the basic jurisprudence for the Church's present law regarding lay brother novices. Canon 564 makes some small but significant changes in that jurisprudence, adapting the pre-Code legislation better to the present needs of the monastic orders, by de-emphasizing the separation of the novitiate in general and stressing the segregation of the *conversi* novices from the others. Paragraph one of canon 564 mitigates §6 of the *Cum ad regularem* by adding the phrase " as far as possible " to the prescription that the novitiate be separated from the rest of the monastery by its own *clausura.* In §2 the canon is stricter than Clement VIII's Constitution, for it says without reservation, " A separate place is to be assigned to the *conversi* novices," whereas the former law spoke only of a separate place for sleeping, and added the concession, " if at all convenient." [12]

The text of the Constitution of Clement VIII shows definitely that in pre-Code law the *conversi* novices were assigned a " separate place " inside the novitiate, and not a place separate from the novitiate. This same idea predominates in the canons of the article under consideration here. Thus Schaefer interprets canon 564, §2: [13]

> The Code supposes that there is formally one novitiate ruled by but one novice master (cf. can. 559, §2, 564, §2, 565, §§1, 2). Although it is legally a unit, so that the novitiate for any one class can not be licitly divided, it is admissible for the novice master to separate it into two sections, in order to instruct the different classes.
>
> If nevertheless the novitiate is as a matter of fact completely separated into two sections, each with its own independent novice master, these cannot be con-

[11] Cans. 553-571.

[12] §15—*Fontes,* n. 189.

[13] *De Religiosis,* n. 245, 9.

> sidered *canonically* as two novitiates (cf. can. 554, §§1, 2, which speaks of the novitiate house).[14]

This interpretation according to the *Cum ad regularem* is contradicted flatly by Prümmer when he speaks of the novitiate *clausura:* [15]

> The novitiate of the *conversi* is to be separate from the novitiate of the clerics.[16]

It is interesting to note here a division of the authors based on their personal membership either in the ancient orders or in the modern institutes of simple vows. Schaefer, a Capuchin, whose opinion is quoted above, is perhaps the only canonist belonging to a medieval order who does not emphasize the need for the separation of the *conversi* novices from the clerical novices. This division of sentiment is further illustrated by a comparison of Augustine's laconic commentary on canon 564, §2: [17]

> Futile reasons are sometimes advanced to abolish this pedagogically sound law,

with the mild views of Vermeersch: [18]

> A less stringent separation is enjoined for the *conversi* novices. They are to be regarded as occupying a separate place if they are segregated from the others at table, at recreation and in the dormitory,

and of Creusen: [19]

---

[14] Cf. also Pejška, *Ius Canonicum Religiosorum* (3. ed., Friburgi Brisgoviae: Herder, 1927), p. 90.

[15] *Manuale Iuris Canonici* (3. ed. Friburgi Brisgoviae: Herder, 1922), q. 211, 2.

[16] Cf. also Blat, *Commentarium,* II, n. 633; Mayer, *Benediktinisches Ordensrecht in der Beuroner Kongregation* (4 vols., Beuron: Kunstverlag, 1929–1936), III, 93. To be cited as *Ordensrecht.*

[17] *Commentary,* III, 240.

[18] *Epitome,* I, n. 712.

[19] Creusen-Garesché-Ellis, *Religious Men and Women in the Code,* n. 206, 3.

> The lay-brother novices may, however, have rather frequent communication with the other novices. Such relations will foster humility and charity.

This whole divergence of opinion results from attempts to interpret one uniform general law to meet the needs of religious institutes which are different in their origin and scope, and which have *conversi* as different from one another as the orders and congregations to which they belong. The monasteries which today retain the cenobitic life with two classes of religious living and working habitually side by side, with every opportunity for mutual observation and envy, need far stricter rules for separation to maintain peace in their communities, than those apostolic institutes whose work takes their members, especially the priests, outside their houses and leaves little time for, and provides a sufficient remedy against, the mutual disedification that can result from the lay brothers' familiar and haphazard association with the clerics. The need for separation is verified also with regard to *conversi* novices, with the added reason in their case of precluding any interference with the special spiritual training they receive from the novice master.

Since the text of canon 564 differs from that of the *Cum ad regularem* from which it is taken, and yet does not clearly establish a change in the law, all of the opinions cited above are admissible,[20] even if they are not all simultaneously applicable to any individual case. Thus Suarez:[21]

> Nor can one cite the customs of other religious institutes by way of example, for there is one Holy Spirit and He has given divergent constitutions to the many and varying communities, according to their several aims and objectives.

In its *Statutes for Extern Sisters* the Sacred Congregation for Religious prescribes:[22]

[20] Can. 6, 3°.

[21] *Tractatus de Religione Societatis Jesu,* lib. VII, cap. II, n. 9.

[22] N. 31—Schaefer, *De Religiosis,* n. 658.

> The canonical novitiate year is to be spent inside the monastery cloister, in the place reserved for the *conversae* novices . . .

The Sacred Congregation's extension of canon 564 is less rigorous therefore than its application of canon 558 in statute 28, cited above.[23] Statute 28 uses the same language as canon 558, adding the sanction of nullity to the law that the novitiate made in preparation for religious profession as nuns, whether choir nuns or *conversae,* does not fulfill the canonical requirement for those aspiring to take vows as extern sisters, and, vice versa, that the novitiate made in preparation for religious profession as extern sisters can not hold good for those who desire to take vows as nuns; whereas statute 31 prescribes that the extern novices are to spend their canonical novitiate year in the same place as the *conversae* novices, although these latter are to be separated from the choir novices. This follows the general intent of the Code's article "On the Training of Novices," which lays greater stress on the separation of the *conversi* novitiate as regards its exclusive training for a specific class, than on the personal separation of the various classes of novices from one another.

## §2. Repetition of the Novitiate Required for the Transfer from One Class to Another

According to canon 558, cited above, a person who has made his novitiate and perhaps pronounced his vows, either as a clerical or as a lay religious, will have to repeat that novitiate if he wants to transfer from the first chosen class to another. This requirement of the Code provides a sufficient obstacle to any hasty and unconsidered change, guarantees the proper separation between the several classes of religious, and thus preserves the *conversi* institute intact. This Code obligation is binding equally upon clerics who want to become *conversi* and upon lay religious who aspire to the reception of Orders. Pre-Code law forbade the latter transfer, which therefore became possible only by dispensation of the Holy See.[24]

---

23 P. 67.

24 Clemens VIII, const. *Cum ad regularem,* 19 mart. 1603, §16—*Fontes,* n. 189; S. C. Ep. et Reg., *Normae* 28 iun. 1901 (Romae, 1901), art. 50.

The joint decree of the Sacred Congregation for Religious and of the Sacred Congregation of Seminaries and Universities, issued on July 25, 1941,[25] does not contemplate those who aspire to membership as *conversi* in religious institutes, except in the case in which those persons abandon their call to the brotherhood and ask to be admitted to the seminary. The decree prescribes that if a candidate for the seminary belonged to a religious community in any way at all, the ordinary has to confer with the Sacred Congregation of Seminaries and Universities before the candidate can be admitted; and conversely, if a candidate for a religious community left a seminary for any cause at all, the religious superior has to have recourse to the Sacred Congregation for Religious before the candidate can be admitted. This second provision of the decree could apparently be extended to those who aspire to become *conversi,* but this would be going beyond the context of the law.[26] The context insinuates, rather, candidates for the clerical state; but the clerical and *conversi* classes are mutually exclusive. This strict interpretation of the decree must be followed, according to canon 19 as compared with canon 538,[27] for its restrictions limit the freedom of those who aspire to the religious state.[28]

Inasmuch as canon 558 accepts the fact of the possible transfer of religious from one class to another, but does not enact detailed regulations which would serve as a guide in this matter, the necessary norms, according to canon 20, are to be sought in the laws made for similar situations. In the case under consideration one must look for these laws in canons 632-636, in Title XIV of the second part of Book II of the Code, for in this title the lawgiver proposes his legislation which governs the transfer of a religious from one religious institute to another.[29] This analogy

[25] *AAS,* XXXIII (1941), 371.

[26] Cf. can. 18.

[27] Cf. *supra,* p. 60.

[82] Frison, "Ex-seminarian and Novice: A Clarification,"—*The Jurist,* VI (1946), 416–418.

[29] Beijersbergen, " De transitu religiosi de una classe ad alteram eiusdem religiosi instituti,"—*Periodica de Re Canonica et Morali utili Praesertim Religiosis et Missionariis* (Brugis, Romae, 1905–), XXVI (1937), 33–37,

does not apply to those details which refer exclusively to the transfer to another religious order or congregation, as illustrated in canon 632, which requires an apostolic indult for this change.

By its silence on the point canon 558 derogates from canon 542, 1°, in the case of a professed religious who transfers to another class, and obviates the necessity of obtaining a dispensation from the Holy See before beginning the new novitiate.[30] Canon 558 thus abrogated the prohibition of Pope Clement VIII's Constitution *Cum ad regularem,*[31] which forbade regular *conversi* to transfer to the clerical class even during their time of probation.[32]

Canon 558 demands a repetition of the novitiate even in those cases wherein the same novice master gave the same instructions to both classes of novices, and wherein the whole routine was the same, for

> the very anticipation of one future state in preference to another has a decisive influence on the spirit that pervades the time of probation.[33]

The new novitiate is required for the validity of the subsequent profession, according to canon 572, §1, 3°. In those institutes whose constitutions prescribe no separation into classes until after the novitiate year is completed, the prescription of canon 558 does not apply.[34]

A cleric who transfers to the status of a lay religious would necessarily have to be reduced to the lay state upon making vows

---

148–154, especially 148–149. To be cited as *Periodica.* Father Beijersbergen's article is very thorough and complete, and is only summarized here.

[30] Goyeneche, "Consultationes,"—*CpR,* III (1922), 11; *CpRM,* XVII (1936), 79; Beijersbergen, *art. cit.,* p. 149.

[31] 19 mart. 1603, §16—*Fontes,* n. 189.

[32] Can. 6, 6°. The General Constitutions of the Order of Friars Minor, approved by the Sacred Congregation for Religious on August 22, 1921, retained the prohibition of the *Cum ad regularem,* §16, in their n. 112—*Regula et Constitutiones Generales Fratrum Minorum* (Ad Claras Aquas [Quaracchi] prope Florentiam: Ex typographia collegii S. Bonaventurae, 1922).

[33] Vermeersch-Creusen, *Epitome,* I, n. 710.

[34] *Loc. cit.;* Schaefer, *De Religiosis,* n. 243.

for this class. If he were in major orders he would need the permission of the Holy See, according to canon 211, §1,[35] and it would be prudent to request this grant at the very beginning of the new novitiate. If he were in minor orders he would not need the permission of the Holy See, but would have to notify the local ordinary according to canon 211, §2. Such a cleric in transferring to the class of lay religious would not be reduced to the lay state during his new novitiate, but only upon voluntarily abandoning the clerical state by taking vows as a lay brother.[36] The local ordinary would be notified immediately before this new religious profession if the cleric were subject to him by reason of incardination in his diocese. But if the religious in question had been promoted to clerical tonsure for the service of his institute, or if, having been ordained a diocesan cleric, he had entered the religious institute, taken perpetual vows, and thus lost his proper diocese,[37] he would not be subject to the local ordinary and would not have to notify him.

Should the clerical novice or religious who transfers to the lay class, take vows, and is thus reduced to the lay state, desire to transfer back again to the clerical state, he is not to receive tonsure again, for this ordination can be received but once and remains forever,[38] but he must obtain the permission of the local ordinary to whom he is subject by virtue of incardination,[39] or of the superior or ordinary of the religious institute, if he is not incardinated in a diocese.[40]

The most common cause for a cleric or a teaching brother to transfer to the *conversi* class is his incapacity for further studies, and there is no difficulty when the religious in question asks for such a change himself, or at least agrees to it.

If, however, he is unwilling to become a *conversus,* and has not yet made perpetual vows, his superior can give him the option of making this transfer only in case he has a just cause for

---

[35] Beijersbergen, *art. cit.,* p. 149.

[36] *Art. cit.,* pp. 35–36.

[37] Can. 585.

[38] Can. 211, §1.

[39] Can. 212, §1.

[40] Beijersbergen, *art. cit.,* p. 37.

dismissing him according to canons 637 or 647.[41] These canons have application for one who is still only in temporary vows. The inability of such a religious to go on with his studies and to perform the duties required of him as a member of his institute, once it is proved, constitutes the grave and just cause demanded by these canons to permit his superior to give him the option of transferring to the *conversi* class or of leaving the religious institute,[42] provided always that this incapacity is neither the result of a sickness contracted after profession, nor a matter which was sufficiently known to the superiors at the time of the profession, precluding fraudulent concealment or misrepresentation on the part of the religious.

If a clerical religious professed with temporary vows, who is called into military service and thus has his vows interrupted,[43] is found upon his return to the institute to be incapable of continuing his studies, his superiors can give him the same option as above, of transferring to the *conversi* class or of leaving the religious order or congregation, inasmuch as the powers of dismissal granted to the superiors by canon 637 are extended by the reply of July 15, 1919, of the Sacred Congregation for Religious to this case also.[44]

It must be noted that the religious who is professed with temporary vows can not in any case be forced to transfer to the new class, inasmuch as canon 558 prescribes a new novitiate in relation to the new class and canon 542, 1°, states that when a person is forced into the novitiate he is admitted invalidly. Religious

---

[41] Ellis, "De Transitu ad aliam eiusdem Religionis Classem,"—*Periodica,* XXV (1936), 103*; Beijersbergen, *art. cit.,* p. 150.

[42] O'Neill, *The Dismissal of Religious in Temporary Vows,* The Catholic University of America Canon Law Studies, n. 166 (Washington, D. C.: The Catholic University of America Press, 1942), pp. 139–141. On p. 140 he says that this incapacity "must not have been detected before the first profession. If this lack of ability was fully known before the making of the first profession then the contract in regard to this point was absolute and not conditional."

[43] S. C. de Religiosis, 15 iul. 1919, ad II—*AAS,* XI (1919), 322.

[44] *AAS,* XI (1919), 322; Ellis, "De Transitu ad aliam eiusdem Religionis Classem,"—*Periodica,* XXV (1936), 103*.

profession in the new class would likewise be invalid if made under duress, according to canon 572, §1, 4°.

A clerical or teaching religious in perpetual vows, however, can not be ordered to transfer to the class of the *conversi*, for, if the novitiate made in relation to one class is not good in relation to the other,[45] then certainly the vows he has made as a member of one group can never bind him to live the life of the other. In this instance, as in the case of the religious who is professed with temporary vows, the superior can give him the option of transferring to the other class only when he is empowered by law to dismiss him from the institute. And the religious in perpetual vows can not be dismissed at all, except in accordance with the rules expressed in canons 649-668, which rules never permit the superiors to take such action merely for the reason that the man in question is unable to go on with his studies. Since a dismissal could follow only upon proof of three grave delicts and all subsequent lack of emendation, it is hard to conceive how the superior could admit the dismissed subject to the *conversi* novitiate in the face of the prescription of canon 538 which requires that the person "be fit to assume the obligations of the religious life."

Goyeneche repeats pre-Code law when he says:[46]

> Since the transfer from the clerical to the lay state, provided that the [perpetually professed] religious in question is not in sacred Orders and there is a just cause for the change, depends solely on the authority of the superiors, this religious could be forced to transfer, especially if this hypothesis were in some way suggested in the constitutions. (Cfr. *Constitutiones* Congregationis Missionariorum F.I.C.B.M.V., 1913, parte I, n. 56, 6º.) For if, as the authors say (Cfr. Petra, Commentaria ad *Const. Apostolicas,* t. IV in const. VIII Eugenii IV, n. 16; Bordoni, *Variae resolutiones,* resol. XXIX, n. 92; Bouix, II, 506; Ferraris, verb. *transitus.*), a prelate can impose this transfer as a punishment for a crime, although the religious be otherwise capable for the work of a cleric, then he is all the more entitled to order this change for a religious who has lost this capacity. Noth-

[45] Can. 558.

[46] "Consultationes,"—*CpR,* III (1922), 83-84.

ing else remains for the religious in question except secularization.

The legislation which Goyeneche cites is not valid, however, under the Code, and the superior cannot impose the transfer he describes, in consequence of canon 558 which prescribes a new novitiate in relation to the new class, and of canon 542, 1°, which states that when a person is forced into the novitiate he is admitted invalidly. Religious profession in the new class would likewise be invalid if made under duress, according to canon 572, §1, 4°. A religious who has made perpetual vows in the clerical class, therefore, remains in this status, according to the Code, despite the fact that his superiors may be obliged by canons 974 and 995, §1, to forbid his promotion to Orders.[47] Goyeneche's opinion can be followed only in those institutes whose constitutions, having received approval since the enactment of the Code, empower the superior to impose the transfer from one class to another.

A clerical religious passing to the lay class does not have to make the postulancy required by canon 539, §1, before his novitiate in his capacity of a prospective *conversus,* for the time he spent in the clerical novitiate suffices for the purpose of the canon. Further, canons 558 and 633, §1, are both silent on the point, although they mention the need for a new novitiate.[48]

The silence of these canons, supported by the express provision of canon 634 regarding the transfer of a perpetually professed religious to another institute, also obviates the need for a repetition of the triennial vows prescribed by canon 574, §1. The superior is enabled by §2 of the same canon, however, to prolong the temporary profession, but not beyond six years. If the religious in question has not completed his three years in temporary vows, they remain in force during the new novitiate and afterward, unless he makes his profession in relation to the new class.[49]

---

[47] Cf. Schaefer, *De Religiosis,* n. 297.

[48] Beijersbergen, "De transitu religiosi de una classe ad alteram eiusdem religiosi instituti,"—*Periodica,* XXVI (1937), 151-152; Goyeneche, "Consultationes,"—*CpRM,* XIX (1938), 14.

[49] Cf. can. 633, §§1, 2.

If he has made annual vows and has not as yet completed his triennium, he renews his temporary vows in relation to the former class in order to fill out the required three years, or to have them continue in force until the end of the new novitiate he is making, after which he takes all his vows, temporary until his triennium has elapsed, and after this perpetual, in relation to the new class.[50]

Goyeneche states[51] that the religious who completes his triennium in temporary vows in relation to the first chosen class before or during his novitiate made in relation to the other group, is bound by the law of canon 575, §1,

> When the time of temporary vows has elapsed, the religious . . . either makes his perpetual profession . . . or returns to the world,[52]

and the rule of canon 577, §1,

> When the time for which vows have been made has elapsed they are to be renewed without delay,[53]

to renew his profession with temporary vows in relation to the former class for the time he is to spend in his novitiate now being made in relation to the latter.

Ellis[54] holds the same view with regard to a religious who transfers to another class upon his return to the institute from military service, giving the same reasons as Goyeneche and citing in addition the prescriptions of the decree *Inter reliquas* issued by the Sacred Congregation for Religious on January 1, 1911,[55]

---

[50] Beijersbergen, *art. cit.*, p. 152.

[51] "Consultationes,"—*CpR,* III (1922), 12; *CpRM,* XVII (1936), 79–80. Coronata seems to hold the same view.—*Institutiones Iuris Canonici* (5 vols., Vol. I, Taurini: Marietti, 1928), I, n. 584.

[52] "Exacto professionis temporariae tempore, religiosus . . . vel emittat perpetuam professionem . . . vel ad saeculum redeat; . . ."

[53] "Elapso tempore ad quod vota sunt nuncupata, renovationi votorum nulla est interponenda mora."

[54] "De Transitu ad aliam eiusdem Religionis Classem,"—*Periodica,* XXV (1936), 103*–104*.

[55] Nn. II, IV—*Fontes,* n. 4408. This decree remains in force since the promulgation of the Code.—S. C. de Religiosis, 15 iul. 1919—*AAS,* XI (1919), 322.

which state that the religious after his return from military service is to take temporary vows for at least a year before pronouncing perpetual vows. This law, however, refers to a religious continuing in his first chosen class, and its purpose, as may readily be seen from the context, is merely to delay perpetual profession, whereas a religious who transfers to a new class and starts his new novitiate for this class has no immediate prospect of taking perpetual vows.

The text and context of the canons and decree cited indicate that all they demand is the continuity of the religious life through the profession of vows on the part of those who have completed their novitiate or the time of their temporary profession, in order that they may go on living in the community. The novitiate required by canon 558 for a religious who transfers from one class to another marks the beginning of an entirely new form of life in religion for the individual in question, with a new status and with new obligations. The sooner the old tie based on the former temporary vows expires the better. Canon 633, §2, legislates thus for those who transfer from one institute to another, stating expressly that the former temporary vows are to be allowed to lapse at their expiration during the novitiate in the new community. Schaefer says,[56] "The one who transfers is a novice and therefore there is no reason for profession." But it would be permissible for such a religious to renew his vows in relation to the former class, and to make them binding until the end of his new novitiate, if he wanted to continue in his possession of the rights attached to that particular religious profession.

Arguing by analogy from canon 633, §1, Beijersbergen says[57] that the obligations of the religious in question are radically double during his second novitiate, as long as his vows taken in relation to the first chosen class remain, but that the rights and duties which accompanied his membership in the former class are suspended insofar as they are incompatible with those of the new class. Since in the law there is no express restriction of the rights of this religious, Beijersbergen is correct when he says, in follow-

[56] *De Religiosis*, n. 536.

[57] *Art. cit.*, p. 154.

ing the norm of canon 19, that he enjoys the full exercise of all his rights, except such as are incompatible with his new status as a novice. His obligations, however, which derive from his membership in the first chosen class, would appear rather to be altogether suspended, since there is no juridical reason for denying the principle of canon 633, §1, regarding the suspension of the duties of the religious novice, whereas the rule of canon 19 presents an obstacle to the application of this same principle regarding his rights.

Arguing once more from analogy, one can state that during his new novitiate the religious in question is to wear the novice's habit of the class to which he is transferring. In fact, the Sacred Congregation for Religious has so decided with regard to a religious who is changing to a new institute and making the novitiate prescribed by canon 633, §1.[58]

Again, if one follow Beijersbergen and Schaefer,[59] the prescription of canon 575, §2, is to be interpreted literally for the religious who transfers to another class in the same institute even after the completion of his temporary vows, so that the vote of the council or the chapter with relation to his admission to perpetual profession is consultative only.

[58] 14 maii 1923—*AAS*, XV (1923), 289.

[59] *Art. cit.*, pp. 153–154; *De Religiosis*, n. 536.

## CHAPTER VI

### EDUCATION AND INSTRUCTION OF *CONVERSI*

As a man thinks, so he acts. He can not want what he does not know. The *conversus* will never love and practice the religious life unless he is given an appreciation of its beauty and value to himself personally by competent and often repeated instruction. He must know *why* he perseveres in the hard life he has chosen, what he is supposed to achieve, and how he is to go about it.[1]

State-supported public high schools, which are open to all in the United States, have given young people in general, and therefore the average *conversi* candidates, all the advantages of a broader and more advanced secular education, together with all the disadvantages of a free and easy disciplinary training, and the delusion that modern progress can change this earth from a place of work and trial to a paradise where everyone is entitled to find and enjoy the happiness he seeks. "Secular standardizing agencies" are also having a detrimental effect on Catholic schools, crowding out Christian training with their required courses, and leaving but the personal example of zealous religious teachers to foster the pupils' spiritual life.[2]

Aspirants to the life of lay religious in our country are therefore richer in their general intellectual development and comparatively more poverty-stricken in their moral training than was usual in the countries where the previous jurisprudence on the direction of *conversi* was developed. That jurisprudence is adapting itself in the United States to meet the problems and to make

[1] Pius XI, epist. apost. *Unigenitus*, 19 mart. 1924—*AAS*, XVI (1924), 147.

[2] Garesché, "The Brothers Carry On but Need Young Recruits,"—*America* (New York: The America Press, 1909–), LXVI (Nov. 29, 1941), 204–205; "Congenial Soil for Vocations,"—*America*, LXVI (Feb. 14, 1942), 511–512; "Influences in our Schools Unfavorable to Religious Vocations," —*The Catholic Mind* (New York: The America Press, 1903–), XL (June 22, 1942), n. 948, 1–6.

use of the opportunities resulting from the situation just described.

The Christian education of a *conversus*, like that of any other religious, begins in the Catholic home. This real education has nothing to do with the broad smattering of knowledge or the encyclopedic ignorance of defective schools, but produces

> . . . the true Christian, . . . the supernatural man who thinks, judges and acts constantly and consistently in accordance with right reason illumined by the supernatural light of the example and teaching of Jesus Christ; in other words, . . . the true and finished man of character . . .[3]

The Code prescribes that Catholic parents give their children this religious and moral training so especially necessary in candidates for religion:

> Parents have a most grave obligation to give their children the best possible *religious* and moral as well as natural and civil *education*, . . .[4]

> All the faithful are from childhood to receive the kind of education which not only shields them from everything that militates against the Catholic religion and decent morals, but likewise recognizes religion and morality as factors so essential that their claims outweigh all other educational considerations.[5]

Inasmuch as the religious life is the perfection of the Christian life in a formal and recognized vocation, the specialized training which prepares a person for his profession of vows and his subsequent perseverance in the monastery to his own spiritual profit, is nothing more than a continuation and an elaboration of the rudiments learned in the home. If these fundamentals are lack-

---

[3] Pius XI, litt. encyc. *Divini illius Magistri*, 31 dec. 1929—*AAS*, XXII (1930), 83.

[4] Can. 1113: "Parentes gravissima obligatione tenentur prolis educationem tum religiosam et moralem, tum physicam et civilem pro viribus curandi, . . ."

[5] Can. 1372, §1: "Fideles omnes ita sunt a pueritia instituendi ut non solum nihil eis tradatur quod catholicae religioni morumque honestati adversetur, sed praecipuum institutio religiosa ac moralis locum obtineat."

ing in a particular case, they must be supplied as soon as possible, and before the subject is advanced to higher instructions:

> This external discipline will lead to a proper character development, . . .
>
> In accord with the decrees of the Holy See, they [the superior of the postulants and the master of novices] shall explain all of Christian doctrine, and especially what pertains to the proper and fruitful reception of the sacraments of Penance and Holy Communion, using as their guide the Catechism of the Council of Trent for pastors. At the same time they shall teach them the obligations they will assume at religious profession and the virtues they must cultivate to lead the life of the vows. . . .[6]

Something more than general instruction in Christian doctrine is needed as soon as the aspirant to the religious life chooses a definite institute for which he wants to prepare and train himself. For each religious organization is different in some respects—be it in the matter of specified prayer, discipline or work—from every other, and each must train its candidates for its own particular way of life. This is part of the purpose of the postulancy and the novitiate,[7] lasting six months and one year respectively, according to the Code,[8] though either or both may be lengthened six months, at the discretion of the major superior.[9]

A new idea, not envisioned in the Code, but entirely in conformity with its prescriptions, is the preparatory school for brothers, such as is conducted by St. Meinrad's Benedictine Abbey, Indiana.[10] The purpose of this school is to prepare young men for the lay brotherhood, just as the scholasticate or minor seminary prepares others to be choir monks and priests. If it offends against the old jurisprudence by taking boys while they are still very young and in their formative years, it follows very well the new trend of the Code, which abolishes former limita-

---

[6] S. C. de Religiosis, decr. *Sacrosancta,* 1 ian. 1911—*Fontes,* n. 4407.

[7] Can. 565, §1.

[8] Cans. 539, §1; 555, §1, 2°.

[9] Cans. 539, §2; 571, §2.

[10] For a detailed description of this school cf. Schaefers, "A Preparatory School for Brothers,"—*ER,* CIII (1940), 67–72.

tions and admits lay brothers at exactly the same age as other religious.[11] Besides the necessary high school subjects, formative training and technical instruction in the crafts and trades receive considerable stress, for fitting the brother "oblates," as they are called, for work that will occupy and develop their talents, such training and instruction being an asset to their own spiritual life as well as to the material good of their community.[12]

### §1. The Postulancy

Although the ultimate purpose of the postulancy in religious institutes, as that of the novitiate, is one of trial and experiment to ascertain the aspirant's vocation,[13] its immediate end is one of instruction and preparation of the candidate for the religious life.[14] The facts that the *conversi* vocation has always been recognized as especially difficult, that lay aspirants have comparatively less previous training and less adaptability,[15] and, what is more important today, that non-clerical candidates for the religious life usually come to the community as total strangers, not having become acquainted with the institute or its members while in the seminary or the scholasticate,[16] as is the case with clerical religious, constitute reasons for the law which supplements the year's novitiate with a six months' postulancy in institutes of perpetual vows. It is a safeguard for the stability of the religious state, for the protection of the professed members, and for the aspirants themselves, to provide an adequate

---

[11] Cans. 555, §1, 1°; 573. Cf. Pius XI, epist. apost. *Unigenitus,* 19 mart. 1924—*AAS,* XVI (1924), 140; Esser, "Comment,"—*Report of the Benedictine Brother Instructors' Convention, 1942,* p. 14.

[12] Esser, Brunsman, Frank, "Comment,"—*Report of the Benedictine Brother Instructors' Convention, 1942,* pp. 15–16.

[13] Can. 571, §2; S. C. de Religiosis, decr. *Quo propositum,* 15 aug. 1912—*Fontes,* n. 4412; St. Benedict, *Rule,* c. 58; Schaefer, *De Religiosis,* nn. 214, 2; 219.

[14] Schaefer, *De Religiosis,* n. 214, 2.

[15] Pejška, *Ius Canonicum Religiosorum,* p. 86.

[16] Creusen-Garesché-Ellis, *Religious Men and Women in the Code,* n. 171; Amhof, "The Training of Novices and Candidates for Our Holy Order,"—*Report of the Benedictine Brother Instructors' Convention, 1942,* pp. 45–46.

time of probation and preparation before recruits in religion are admitted to vows.[17]

The law is stated in canon 539, §1:

> In religious institutes of perpetual vows all women, and, in communities of men, the *conversi,* are to make a postulancy of at least six whole months before they are admitted to the novitiate; in religious organizations of merely temporary vows, however, the respective constitutions are to be observed regarding both the necessity and the duration of the postulancy; [18]

and in canon 540, §1:

> The postulancy is to be made under the special supervision of a tried and tested religious in the novitiate or in another house of the institute where the discipline is well kept according to the constitutions.[19]

The six months' postulancy is nearly as old as the *conversi* institute.[20] The postulancy of two years required by the decree *Sacrosancta* [21] for the validity of the subsequent profession of *conversi* professed with solemn vows has been abrogated by canon 539, §1. The postulancy of six months as prescribed by this canon is, moreover, not demanded for the *validity* either of the novitiate or of the profession that follows.[22] The canon is binding only on those lay brothers who are *conversi,* that is, on those who form a second class in their institutes; hence other lay brothers are not required to make a postulancy before their

[17] Cf. S. C. de Religiosis, decr. *Quo propositum,* 15 aug. 1912—*Fontes,* n. 4412.

[18] "In religionibus a votis perpetuis mulieres omnes et, si agatur de religione virorum, conversi, antequam ad novitiatum admittantur, postulatum ad sex saltem integros menses peragant; in religionibus vero a votis temporariis, ad necessitatem et tempus postulatus quod attinet, standum constitutionibus."

[19] "Postulatus peragi debet vel in domo novitiatus vel in alia religionis domo in qua disciplina secundum constitutiones accurate servetur sub speciali cura probati religiosi."

[20] Cf. Martène-Durand, *Thesaurus,* IV, 1327, n. 2; 1338, n. 1.

[21] S. C. de Religiosis, 1 ian. 1911, n. 2—*Fontes,* n. 4407.

[22] Schaefer, *De Religiosis,* n. 214, 5; Oesterle, *Praelectiones,* I, 283.

novitiate.[23] This interpretation finds support in the wording of the Instruction and the Decree of the Sacred Congregation for Religious, of November 25, 1929, addressed to the superiors and superioresses general of lay religious institutes, which deal with their obligation to imbue their subjects properly with Christian doctrine.[24] This new decree, without mentioning canon 539 or the term *conversi*, enacts special rules for the instruction and examination in Christian doctrine of all the aspirants to membership in lay religious institutes, and thus leaves intact the traditional use of *conversi* as a technical term which is never to be extended to include all lay religious. Indeed, lay religious institutes may have a separate class of *conversi*. The 1929 decree does not apply to *conversi* postulants in clerical institutes, inasmuch as it is addressed only to the superiors of lay religious institutes.

Although the Code and subsequent decrees do not bind superiors to instruct *conversi* postulants as such [25] in Christian doctrine, canon law reminded these superiors of their serious obligation to do so, in the pre-Code decree *Sacrosancta*,[26] which was neither abrogated nor derogated by the silence of canons 539-541, and of the decree of November 25, 1929. Indeed, since canon 509, §2, 2°, requires it for the professed *conversi* and canon 565, §2, prescribes it for the *conversi* novices, analogy of law [27] would indicate its necessity for the postulants.

## §2. The Novitiate

The novitiate is a time of probation to ascertain the vocation

[23] Schaefer, *De Religiosis*, n. 214, 4; Vermeersch-Creusen, *Epitome*, I, n. 665; Oesterle, *Praelectiones*, I, 283–284. Prümmer *(Manuale Iuris Canonici*, q. 203) errs in extending the obligation which is mentioned in can. 539, §1, to all *conversi*, for the canon plainly states that in institutes of merely temporary vows the postulancy depends on the prescriptions of the constitutions.

[24] *AAS*, XXII (1930), 28–29.

[25] Those who are in lay religious institutes fall under the instruction and the decree here discussed. Cf. S. C. de Religiosis, 25 nov. 1929—*AAS*, XXII (1930), 28–29.

[26] S. C. de Religiosis, 1 ian. 1911—*Fontes*, n. 4407.

[27] Cf. can. 20.

and fitness of the aspirant for the religious life.[28] Its immediate end is stated in canon 565, §1:

> The novitiate year spent under the novice master must have as its purpose the spiritual formation of the candidate, through the study of the rule and the constitutions, through pious meditations and assiduous prayer, through the mastery of what is necessary for the keeping of the vows and the conduct of a virtuous life, through exercises and practices calculated to uproot completely the seedlings of vice, to discipline the affections, and to facilitate the acquisition of the virtues.[29]

Canon 565 emphasizes a more comprehensive Christian education for *conversi* in §2:

> Besides this, the *conversi* [novices] are to be instructed diligently in Christian doctrine, with a special conference for them at least once a week.[30]

The decree *Sacrosancta*[31] remains the classic source for a description of the training and the instruction which are to be given to *conversi* novices.[32]

A further obligation, going beyond the prescription of canon 565, §2, is laid on *conversi* novices in lay religious institutes by the Instruction and the Decree of the Sacred Congregation for Religious, dated November 25, 1929.[33] This Instruction and Decree prescribe the following:

> 1. During their probationship and noviceship the

[28] Cans. 563, 571, §2.

[29] "Annus novitiatus debet sub disciplina Magistri hoc habere propositum, ut informetur alumni animus studio regulae et constitutionum, piis meditationibus assiduaque prece, iis perdiscendis quae ad vota et ad virtutes pertinent, exercitationibus opportunis ad vitiorum semina radicitus extirpanda, ad compescendos animi motus, ad virtutes acquirendas."

[30] "Conversi praeterea diligenter in christiana doctrina instituantur, speciali collatione ad eos habita semel saltem in hebdomada."

[31] S. C. de Religiosis, 1 ian. 1911—*Fontes,* n. 4407. Cf. the lengthy extracts translated above, pp. 43–49.

[32] Pejška, *Ius Canonicum Religiosorum,* p. 96.

[33] *AAS,* XXII (1930), 28–29.

> young men and women shall review their Christian doctrine and learn it more thoroughly, so that each one shall not only know it by heart but also be able to explain it correctly; nor shall they be admitted to take the vows without a sufficient knowledge thereof, and a previous examination.[34]

The subsequent numbers of the decree apply only to those lay religious who are to teach Christian doctrine in schools or parishes. If, by way of exception, the *conversi* in lay religious institutes should be assigned such work, they have to conform also to these prescriptions.

The Sacred Congregation for Religious has always insisted that the novices have a complete copy, and not a mere summary, of the rule and the constitutions.[35]

Canon 565 in §3 legislates for the effectiveness of the novitiate by putting the following ban on hindrances to the aspirant's instruction and probation:

> During the novitiate year . . . the *conversi* must stay at home in the religious house and perform only such tasks of the lay brothers (always in a subordinate capacity) as will not occasion any hindrance in the exercises prescribed for the novitiate.[36]

What comprises the "exercises prescribed for the novitiate" is detailed in §1 of this same canon. If the *conversi* novices are considered as candidates for the religious life, and not as unpaid workmen whose services may be exploited by the institution, they will be made to labor, during the year preceding their profession of vows, for a period somewhat shorter than the usual eight hours of the working day. They are not to act as functionaries

[34] This translation is reproduced from Bouscaren, *The Canon Law Digest* (2 vols., Milwaukee: Bruce, 1934–1943), I, 281.

[35] Instr. 25 mart. 1922, n. 18—*AAS,* XIV (1922), 279; Schaefer, *De Religiosis,* n. 246; Fanfani, *De Iure Religiosorum* (2. ed., Romae: Marietti, 1925), n. 198, B.

[36] "Anno novitiatus . . . conversi autem in ipsa religiosa domo eatenus tantum fungi possunt officiis fratrum conversorum (non tamen uti primarii officiales), quatenus ab exercitiis novitiatus pro ipsis constitutis non praepediantur."

with primary responsibility, e.g., as the porter, the tailor or the cook, for the character of their motive in joining the monastery still remains to be ascertained—whether it be a supernatural one, as is required in religious, or perhaps merely a natural or even selfish one.[37] A novice without a manifestly supernatural vocation is not to be admitted to vows. His material usefulness to the community is not enough reason to vindicate his membership in the institute.

The prescription of canon 564, §1, that the novices be segregated as much as possible from the professed religious, without any interassociation except for a special reason and with the permission of the superior or of the novice master, is especially important in the training of *conversi*. The reason that violations of this canon are so disastrous to vocations is that the confidences of professed religious, who seek the company of newcomers when they are dissatisfied with that of their own confrères, are a real scandal[38] to untried souls which are not yet activated with solid religious principles.

## §3. The Spiritual Training of the Professed Brothers

With the promulgation of the Code a number of the recommendations of the decree *Sacrosancta* were embodied in the law of the Church, in canon 509, §2:

> Local superiors are to provide:
>
> 1°. That at least once a year, on fixed days, the constitutions of the community be read publicly, as also the decrees which the Holy See shall prescribe to be read in public.
>
> 2°. That at least twice a month, in keeping with the prescription of canon 565, §2, an instruction in Christian doctrine be held for the *conversi* and domestic servants, adapted to their understanding, and also, especially in non-clerical religious institutes, a pious exhortation for all the members of the house.[39]

---

[37] Becnel, "The Brothers and their Work,"—*Report of the Benedictine Brother Instructors' Convention, 1942,* p. 84.

[38] Cf. *Matth.,* XVIII, 6.

[39] "Curent Superiores locales:

"1°. Ut saltem semel in anno, statis diebus, publice legantur propriae

It is not the mind of the Church to keep religious ignorant of what canon law prescribes in their regard. The individual religious have the right and the duty to know the norms by which they are governed, and each must have a copy of his constitutions.[40]

As to the latter part of number one (1°) quoted above, all legislation applying to lay religious is to be read in the vernacular, and, if necessary, explained and recommended for observance. Since the promulgation of the Code the Holy See has so far not prescribed the public reading before the *conversi* of any particular decree.[41] The only documents which, as communications to be read publicly in the community, have been issued since the enactment of the Code, are the instruction of the Sacred Congregation for Religious, of December 1, 1931, regarding the studies and examinations in preparation for the priesthood, which has to be read only to clerical religious,[42] and the lengthy statutes prescribed by the same Sacred Congregation for the extern sisters in monasteries of nuns, which are to be read in their entirety to these sisters at least four times a year.[43]

The prescription of canon 565, §2, referred to in number two of canon 509,. §2, is that *conversi* novices are to have a special conference in Christian doctrine at least once a week. The present canon prescribes the continuation of this "instruction in Christian doctrine . . . at least twice a month" for the professed *conversi*. The obligations of the two canons can be fulfilled by a joint conference for both groups, but it may often be better to instruct the novices and the professed separately.[44] Like the *conversi* novices mentioned in canon 565, §2, so the professed *conversi* spoken of in canon 509, §2, 2°, include only those who

---

constitutiones, itemque decreta quae publice legenda Sancta Sedes praescribet;

"2°. Ut saltem bis in mense, firmo praescripto can. 565, §2, christianae catechesis habeatur instructio pro conversis et familiaribus, audientium conditioni accommodata, et, praesertim in religionibus laicalibus, pia ad omnes de familia exhortatio."

[40] S. C. de Religiosis, instr. 25 mart. 1922, n. 18—*AAS,* XIV (1922), 279.

[41] Schaefer, *De Religiosis,* nn. 144 and 144 bis.

[42] *AAS,* XXIV (1932), 74-81. Cf. *Periodica,* XXI (1932), 187.

[43] 16 iul. 1931, n. 127—Schaefer, *De Religiosis,* n. 669.

[44] Schaefer, *De Religiosis,* n. 144 bis.

constitute a second, non-clerical class in their institutes.[45] But also as in the case of canon 565, §2, an independent later prescription, without making any reference to the canon, enacted a similar rule for all other lay brothers. This is found in Pope Pius XI's Apostolic Letter *Unigenitus:*

> . . . But most of all the superiors are not to neglect the instruction of the lay brothers, either personally or through priests who are properly qualified, in the eternal and sublime truths of the faith, which if known and frequently called to mind furnish many incentives to virtue for any man, whether living in the world or within monastery walls. We wish these things which we have just said to be applied also to all the members of lay congregations, for it is especially necessary that these receive a higher instruction in religion, which goes beyond what is ordinarily taught the faithful, inasmuch as these religious frequently devote themselves to the education of children and adolescents.[46]

The "domestic servants" mentioned in canon 509, §2, 2°, are lay people who live in the religious house day and night, and work for the community. Yet weighty authorities who have made a special study of the problem include also those who are mentioned in canon 514, §1, namely those who live in the house as students, guests or patients.[47]

The "pious exhortation" prescribed in the second part of canon 509, §2, 2°, is to be distinguished from the "instruction in Christian doctrine" required in the first part. The "exhortation" is for "all the members of the house." It is disputed whether this phrase includes only the members of the religious community, or whether it is to be extended also to others living in the house. All agree, however, that all the *conversi,* novices as well as professed, are bound to attend the exhortation.[48]

In a lay institute both the catechetical instruction and the pious exhortation may be given by such of its members as are com-

[45] *Loc. cit.*

[46] *AAS*, XVI (1924), 147.

[47] Schaefer, *De Religiosis,* n. 144 bis.

[48] *Loc. cit.*

petent, whether by the superiors or by those whom they designate; or a priest, even an outsider, may be called in for the purpose. Creusen states: [49]

> If *need be,* the parish clergy may be asked to give the catechetical instruction. If the convent has *no chaplain* who can give exhortations, the domestics of the house ought to be sent, *whenever possible,* to the parochial Mass. . . . In lay congregations an effort should be made to have some priest give exhortations, at least from time to time. . . . The fact that priests are not available *will excuse superiors for omitting a certain number of instructions.*

It is possible to join the instruction and the exhortation, both being given together, and thus to satisfy the twofold obligation of the canon,[50] but neither is a substitute for the other.

Although the phrase "adapted to their understanding" is applied by canon 509 to the first prescription of §2, 2°, namely, the catechetical instruction, it is here treated last because of the longer commentary it suggests. The phrase is of necessity giving rise to a new jurisprudence in the United States, for the "understanding" of our lay brothers, with whom literacy is the rule and not the exception, offers opportunities for development not enjoyed by the lay brothers of former days in other lands:

> The junior brothers resent it when an "oblate" candidate is admitted who is comparatively illiterate. A man whose mind is developed makes twice as good a religious.[51]

At the same time, the lay brothers have not received the advanced and comprehensive theological training given to clerics, but they

> . . . lead simple lives, taking the word of instruc-

[49] Creusen-Garesché-Ellis, *Religious Men and Women in the Code,* n. 87. Italics inserted by the present writer.

[50] Schaefer, *De Religiosis,* n. 144 bis; Vermeersch-Creusen, *Epitome,* I, n. 629.

[51] Brunsman, "Comment,"—*Report of the Benedictine Brother Instructors' Convention, 1942,* p. 15.

> tion . . . very directly and carrying it out to the letter. Their needs are few and uniform. Do not misunderstand me: when I say "simple," I do not mean "ignorant." The brothers may be comparatively unlettered (so was St. Benedict: *scienter nescius et sapienter indoctus*), but they are more wise in spiritual things, more able to assimilate deep spiritual truths based on religious experience, more ready for advance in perfection than we realize. . . .
>
> Their mode of life has not only advantages but also obstacles that are distinctive. I should like to stress two: the tendency to become passive spiritually, to go on receiving without giving out, and the tendency to become mechanical in their exercises. . . . The problem, then, is how to activate them spiritually, . . .[52]

The brother's spiritual reading is another very important element in his religious development. This is also explained at some length by Father Botz in the article just cited:

> . . . Like instruction, this [sacred reading] is of prime importance for brothers after their profession, in order to prepare them for prayer and to nourish prayer and meditation. . . . If this reading is to remain sacred, it should include primarily the Sacred Scriptures. . . . Surely, some guidance is needed, both as to what to read and how to interpret; this guidance should be available from a father in the community and might help to combine instruction and reading. Then there are the writings of the Fathers (now printed in the St. Meinrad breviary translations) . . .[53]
>
> . . . Even for the professed brothers spiritual reading should be directed in a general way at least, so that valuable time will not go to forbidden or useless reading, or even too much browsing in secondary handbooks of devotion.[54]

---

[52] Botz, "The Spiritual Direction of Professed Brothers,"—*Report of the Benedictine Brother Instructors' Convention, 1942,* pp. 103–106.

[53] *The Lessons of the Temporal Cycle and the Principal Feasts of the Sanctoral Cycle according to the Monastic Breviary, compiled and adapted for the Office of the Brothers of St. Meinrad's Abbey* (St. Meinrad, Indiana: The Abbey Press, 1941).

[54] Botz, *art. cit.,* pp. 107–109.

Fidelity to spiritual reading has a direct relation to perseverance:

> As to spiritual reading, boys with an intellectual tendency are good readers, and will devote more time to it than the required half hour. The older brothers note that candidates will not persevere unless they love their reading.[55]

Later in his article Father Botz speaks of mortification:

> . . . Self-training in voluntary self-denial must continue during the time of vows even more than before. Again, training is imperative in order to bring the voluntary practises in line with obedience, since we believe that mortification is a relative good and not an end in itself. Without such voluntary self-denial, the monastic life of a brother readily degenerates into following the line of least resistance. . . .
>
> . . . Finally, the amount of direction and correction depends largely on the extent of self-accusation or manifestation.[56]

Study clubs may provide an opportunity to induce lay brothers to pursue their spiritual reading with more fruit and understanding. Such a plan proved useful at St. Meinrad's Benedictine Abbey, Indiana:

---

[55] Brunsman, "Comment,"—*Report of the Benedictine Brother Instructors' Convention, 1942,* p. 86. Cf. also p. 98.

[56] *Art. cit.,* pp. 112–113. Cf. can. 530: "§1. Omnes religiosi Superiores districte vetantur personas sibi subditas quoquo modo inducere ad conscientiae manifestationem sibi peragendam.

"§2. Non tamen prohibentur subditi quominus libere ac ultro aperire animum suum Superioribus valeant; imo expedit ut ipsi filiali cum fiducia Superiores adeant, eis, si sint sacerdotes, dubia quoque et anxietates suae conscientiae exponentes."

"§1. All religious superiors are strictly forbidden to induce their subjects in any way to make a manifestation of conscience to them.

"§2. The subjects however are not forbidden freely and of their own accord to open their minds to their superiors; indeed, it is expedient for them to approach their superiors with filial confidence and, if the latter are priests, to reveal to them also the doubts and the anxieties of conscience."

During the past Lent a study club for the Junior Brothers and novices was a great success. We studied the sacraments. Some read two or three books. Very fine papers were prepared and read before all the brothers without embarrassment. They were followed by a discussion sometimes of half an hour.[57]

[57] Brunsman, "Comment,"—*Report of the Benedictine Brother Instructors' Convention, 1942,* p. 88.

# CHAPTER VII

## *ORA ET LABORA*

### §1. The Duty Prayers of the "Conversi"

Their exemption from the obligation of reciting the divine office in choir is a distinguishing characteristic of the *conversi,* and their vocation has always been regarded as the counterpart of that of choir religious. This is the law of canon 610:

> §1. In religious institutes, either of men or of women, which have the choir obligation, in each house where there are at least four religious who are obligated by the choir duty, or even fewer if the constitutions so prescribe, and who are not at the same time lawfully hindered, the divine office must be recited daily in common according to the constitutions. . . .
>
> §3. In these same religious institutes, either of men or of women, the solemnly professed, except the *conversi,* who have not been in choir, must recite the canonical hours privately.[1]

The divine office spoken of here comprises the public recitation of the canonical hours of the Breviary and the public celebration of the conventual Mass described in canon 413, §2, as modified for religious by canon 610, §2, and the directives of the Sacred Congregation of Rites.[2]

---

[1] "§1. In religionibus sive virorum sive mulierum, quibus est chori obligatio, in singulis domibus ubi quatuor saltem sint religiosi choro obligati et actu legitime non impediti, et etiam pauciores, si ita ferant constitutiones, debet ad normam constitutionum quotidie divinum officium communiter persolvi. . . .

"§3. In eisdem religionibus sive virorum sive mulierum, sollemniter professi qui a choro abfuerunt, debent, exceptis conversis, horas canonicas privatim recitare."

[2] 2 dec. 1891; 2 maii 1924; 28 febr. 1925—*Decreta Authentica Congrega-*

Their special vocation not only exempts the *conversi* from the duty of reciting the divine office, but it also makes them incapable of satisfying the community's choir obligation according to the law of the Church. This traditional doctrine is but a logical consequence following upon the concept of their definite position, training and activity in their institutes, in contrast to the vocation of choir religious.[3] This does not mean, though, that the law excludes them from choir. Indeed, canon 595, §1, 2°, orders that all religious not lawfully hindered, daily attend Mass, practice mental prayer, and take part diligently in the other devotions prescribed by the rules and constitutions.

The Code thus specifies no duty prayers for the *conversi,* but orders those which are required by the constitutions to be said. In this matter, as with regard to their spiritual training, a new jurisprudence is developing to keep pace with the more advanced education now enjoyed by *conversi.* The evolution of the lay brothers' duty prayers may be traced from the *Paters* of the twelfth century to such a rich and carefully composed office in the vernacular as that printed for the *conversi* of St. John's Benedictine Abbey in Minnesota.[4] St. Meinrad's Benedictine Abbey in Indiana pioneered in this field in the United States, giving its brothers an abridgment of the large breviary:

> . . . This more generous prayer life has been especially fostered in the junior brothers, stressing for them the same benefits of the liturgical life enjoyed by the choir monks. For this purpose an epitome was made of the large choir office to give the "liturgical flavor of each day's feast," in contrast to the Little Office of the Blessed Virgin used by the senior brothers, which changes very little during the course of the year. . . .

---

*tionis Sacrorum Rituum* (6 vols., Romae: Typis Polyglottis Vaticanis, 1898–1927), nn. 3757, 4392, 4393. The last two references may be found also in *AAS,* XVI (1924), 248–249; XVII (1925), 159.

[3] Fanfani, *De Iure Religiosorum,* n. 396; Mayer, *Ordensrecht,* III, 292; Prümmer, *Manuale Iuris Canonici,* q. 235, 1; Schaefer, *De Religiosis,* n. 367; Vermeersch-Creusen, *Epitome,* I, n. 768.

[4] *A Short Breviary for Religious and the Laity* (2. ed., Collegeville, Minnesota: The Liturgical Press, 1942). This breviary is also used by the brothers at Mt. Angel Benedictine Abbey in Oregon.

> The office is noticed to have a profound influence on the brothers' daily lives.[5]

Since canon 595, §1, 2°, prescribes that religious are bound to their duty prayers as specified by their constitutions, these statutes will have to be modified in some cases and submitted for approval to the Sacred Congregation for Religious, to legalize the new offices being introduced.

Unless the contrary is stated in a special precept or in the rules or constitutions of their institutes, *conversae* of simple vows and *conversi* are not bound under pain of grave sin to recite the office or prayers prescribed for them.[6]

> In some congregations of men and in the greater number of the congregations of women, the constitutions prescribe the common recitation of the Little Office of the Blessed Virgin. . . . The Code neither specifies nor increases the obligation of the rule. The Holy See has even forbidden several times that this recitation should be imposed under pain of sin. To omit it, therefore, will not be a sin, except by reason of the motive or the circumstances of this negligence.[7]

*Conversae* of solemn vows who are bound by their constitutions to recite the Little Office of the Blessed Virgin have an *obligatio levis* to do so.[8]

Regarding the "mental prayer" prescribed in the same number two of canon 595, §1, the decree *Sacrosancta*[9] has some remarks that are to the point:

> Care must therefore be taken that the lay brothers . . . for the full time prescribed in the constitutions of their Order . . . devote themselves to prayer alone. It is not enough for them to make their meditation while they are serving Mass.

[5] Esser, "Introduction,"—*Report of the Benedictine Brother Instructors' Convention, 1942,* pp. 2-3.

[6] Prümmer, *Manuale Iuris Canonici,* q. 238.

[7] Creusen-Garesché-Ellis, *Religious Men and Women in the Code,* n. 299. Cf. Augustine, *Commentary,* III, 329: "Not . . . a strict duty."

[8] S. Poenit., resp. 26 oct. 1858—Vermeersch-Creusen, *Epitome,* I, n. 768.

[9] S. C. de Religiosis, 1 ian. 1911—*Fontes,* n. 4407.

The annual retreat, the daily attendance at Holy Mass, the weekly confession and frequent communion;[10] and, by virtue of canon 592, the daily visiting of the Blessed Sacrament, the recitation of the rosary, and the examination of conscience mentioned in canon 125, 2°, constitute in their fulfillment spiritual treasures which the *conversi* enjoy along with all other religious, and need no special comment.

The *conversi's* prayer life is admirably eulogized in the words of Pope Pius XI:[11]

> . . . For the rest, since these lay brothers or *conversi* are exempted by their vocation from the dangers that sometimes threaten religious priests because of the very sublimity of their office, and yet enjoy very similar spiritual privileges and safeguards, which their institute with maternal solicitude is accustomed to bestow on all her children without distinction, it is just that they hold the heavenly gift of their vocation in very high esteem and return the favor to God with grateful will, by often renewing their determination, made on the day of profession, of living up to their calling until death.—We can not refrain here, dearly beloved sons, from exhorting you to reflect on what a grave duty you have of watching that the *conversi,* both during their novitiate and throughout their lives, be furnished with the spiritual helps they need to go forward and persevere, these helps being perhaps the greater in proportion to the lowliness of their status and the humble work they have to do. . . .

## §2. The "Conversi" and their Work

In the same document Pope Pius XI continued:

> For this reason, superiors, in deciding where each one of them is to be stationed and what work he is to do, must consider each individual's talents, and the obstacles that may perhaps confront him. . . .

"The greatest problems of the brotherhood seem to arise in

[10] Cf. S. C. Sacr., instr. 8 dec. 1938—Bouscaren, *The Canon Law Digest,* II, 208-215.

[11] Epist. apost. *Unigenitus,* 19 mart. 1924—*AAS,* XVI (1924), 147.

one way or another from the work question. Either the brothers themselves are not willing to make the proper sacrifices or the first interest of other members in brothers centers in their work."[12] The reasons for the difficulties regarding the work of the *conversi* lie in the widespread application of two contrary principles, both of them representing extreme views, and both of them false. The one side, which has almost become traditional, deriving from the *conversi's* institution in the medieval orders as auxiliary religious, insists that they must in every case adapt themselves to the work that needs to be done, usually cleaning the house and rooms, minding the door, and the like; then, whatever the talents or aptitudes of the religious in question, he must find his happiness and holiness in sacrificing himself to the common good. The other extreme, which is revolutionary, rebels against the idea of an auxiliary status, inasmuch as its proponents want the *conversi* to have a direct and equal share in the general works of the institute. Neither view is realistic or canonical.

The correct and true principle governing the work of the lay brothers may be formulated thus: as full-fledged members of their communities the *conversi* are destined by their proper vocation to do manual work in the same way that choir monks are deputed to the performance of the liturgy, or teaching brothers to the diffusion of Christian education.[13] The basic twofold purpose of the activity of each is the same: to contribute in his own way to the objective progress and growth of the kingdom of God on earth; and by his work, as by his prayer, to attain

[12] *Report of the Benedictine Brother Instructors' Convention, 1942,* p. 73.

[13] Cf. *Consuetudines Hirsaugienses,* lib. II, cc. 11, 22—*MPL,* CL, 1049, 1070; *Vita Beati Wilhelmi, Observationes praeviae,* n. 5—Mabillon, *Acta SS. O.S.B., saec. VI,* P. II, p. 717; reprinted in *MPL,* CL, 892-893; *Vita Willihelmi Abbatis Hirsaugiensis* auctore Heymone, n. 23—*MGH SS,* XII, 219-220; *Exordium parvum,* c. 15—Guignard, *Les monuments,* p. 77; Smet, "The Origin of the Carmelite Laybrothers,"—*The Sword,* VI (1942), 129, 131-132; Benedictus XIV, decr. 21 mart. 1747—Bizzarri, *Coll. S. C. Ep. et Reg.,* pp. 407-409; Clemens VIII, const. *Cum ad regularem,* 19 mart. 1603, §16—*Fontes,* n. 189; S. C. de Religiosis, decr. *Sacrosancta,* 1 ian. 1911—*Fontes,* n. 4407; Pius XI, epist. apost. *Unigenitus,* 19 mart. 1924—*AAS,* XVI (1924), 146-147.

to personal holiness. If the work assigned to religious ever fails to accomplish these ends it is their superiors' duty to make whatever changes may be necessary for it to achieve its purpose.[14]

It is being recognized that in many cases *conversi* will have to be trained in some definite craft or line of work to equip them to perform the labors to be assigned by obedience in a way that will contribute to their spiritual development.[15] Knowles failed to note the progress that has been made in this direction when he wrote a few years ago: [16]

> . . . It was thus a hard life of extreme simplicity, and presupposed the existence of a large class of men wholly illiterate. In England at the present day it is hard to reconstruct even in the imagination the social conditions of the twelfth century, but in the rural districts of south Germany and elsewhere in Europe lay brothers in great numbers may still be found living the same life of absolute simplicity. In the early twelfth century the appeal made by this vocation to the illiterate, who had for many centuries been neglected by monasticism, was immediate and widespread.

This dictum is misleading because the "simple" life of the south German lay brothers is one of highly developed craftsmanship,[17] with many skilled tradesmen and not a few artists among the *conversi*.

Canon 596 prescribes:

> All religious shall wear the proper habit of their institute both inside and outside the house, unless a grave cause should excuse them, according to the judgment of the major superior, or, in case of necessity, the local superior.[18]

---

[14] Cf. Becnel, "The Brothers and Their Work," and Amhof, Bodmayr, Behrman, Brunsman, Esser, Frank, "Comment,"—*Report of the Benedictine Brother Instructors' Convention, 1942*, pp. 74-88.

[15] Bodmayr, "Social and Spiritual Relations of Brothers with Clerical Members,"—*op. cit.*, p. 137.

[16] *The Monastic Order in England*, p. 215.

[17] Butzbach, *Wanderbüchlein* (Leipzig, 1912), *passim*.

[18] "Religiosi omnes proprium suae religionis habitum deferant tum intra tum extra domum, nisi gravis causa excuset, iudicio Superioris maioris aut, urgente necessitate, etiam localis."

In many religious institutes particular law or custom assigns a special habit to the *conversi*, different from that of the other religious in the same community. Pejška says that there should not be a prominently notable difference between the habits of the clerical and the lay religious.[19] St. Meinrad's Benedictine Abbey in Indiana has

> introduced a " work habit " for the Junior Brothers to wear while working. This habit is washable, has a scapular and apron front. They like it very much and it looks neat. Formerly all the brothers ran about the monastery all day without the habit. They looked like lay people all day, and I suppose they felt like them. . . .[20]

[19] *Ius Canonicum Religiosorum*, p. 150.

[20] *Report of the Benedictine Brother Instructors' Convention, 1942*, p. 72.

# CONCLUSIONS

1. The modern *conversi* institute has none of the juridical structure of the ancient lay monastic communities. Cf. pp. 1, 57–58.

2. The twelfth century idea of the *ordo conversorum* existing distinct and separate from the *ordo monachorum* was derived largely from feudal caste distinction in secular Christian society. It came to the *conversi* institute by natural accretion, and was not found at Hirsau, where the distinction was expressly based on the ability to discharge choir duties. It was not founded on the ecclesiastical hierarchy that distinguishes the *ordo laicus* from the *ordo sacerdotalis*. Cf. pp. 15, 20–24, 55–56.

3. The term *conversi*, as used in the Code, is to be defined as the name for a second, non-clerical or non-monastic group of religious whose main work is manual labor, in institutes admitting of more than one class of members. This status is determined solely by the particular rules or constitutions. Cf. pp. 56–58.

4. In legislating for *conversi* the Code has preserved certain inviolable principles which have been proved by the practical experience of the centuries to be the necessary foundations for a jurisprudence for the institute, namely:

(a) In communities with more than one class of members a clear-cut distinction between these classes is prescribed, as well as a separate training of the novices aspiring to membership in each of them. Cf. pp. 66–70, 72.

(b) The dignity of professed brothers as members of the religious state is expressly recognized and vindicated. Cf. pp. 28–32, 50–54.

(c) The need of special religious instruction and training for *conversi* is emphasized. Cf. pp. 40–49, 84–93.

(d) Their exemption from the obligation of reciting the divine office is retained. Cf. pp. 20–22, 97–98.

5. The Code introduces several important innovations into the Canon Law for *conversi;* namely:

(a) It specifies a uniform age for admission to religion for all candidates, including *conversi*. Cf. pp. 60–61.

(b) It makes the rule uniform for the transfer between classes in religious institutes, abolishing the pre-Code prohibition forbidding *conversi* to transfer, even during their time of probation, to the clerical class. Cf. pp. 72–74.

(c) It makes the law for *conversae* the same as that for the *conversi*, except in such matters as the dowry and the observance of the cloister, for which there are special prescriptions for communities of women religious. Cf. pp. 65, 71–72.

## BIBLIOGRAPHY

### SOURCES

*Acta Apostolicae Sedis, Commentarium Officiale,* Romae, 1909–

*Acta Sanctae Sedis,* 41 vols., Romae, 1865–1908.

*Acta Sanctorum* edita cura Ioannis Bollandi et Bollandianorum, Parisiis-Bruxellis, 1863– .

Albers, Bruno, *Consuetudines Monasticae,* 5 vols., Stuttgart-Montis Casini, 1900–1912.

Bouscaren, T. Lincoln, *The Canon Law Digest,* 2 vols., Milwaukee: Bruce, 1934–1943.

*Canonical Legislation concerning Religious,* authorised English translation, Rome, 1919.

*Codex Iuris Canonici Pii X Pontificis Maximi iussu digestus Benedicti Papae XV auctoritate promulgatus,* ed. Petri Card. Gasparri, Romae: Typis Polyglottis Vaticanis, 1917 (Reimpressio, 1934).

*Codicis Iuris Canonici Fontes cura Emi Petri Card. Gasparri editi,* 9 vols., Romae (postea Civitate Vaticana): Typis Polyglottis Vaticanis, 1923–1939. (Vols. VII–IX ed. cura et studio Emi Iustiniani Card. Serédi.)

*Collectanea in usum Secretariae Sacrae Congregationis Episcoporum et Regularium,* ed. 1. et 2. Bizzarri, Romae, 1863 et 1885.

*Corpus Iuris Canonici,* ed. Lipsiensis 2. instruxit Aemilius Friedberg, 2 vols., Lipsiae, 1879–1881. Editio anastatice repetita, 1922.

*Corpus Scriptorum Ecclesiasticorum Latinorum,* editum consilio et impensis Academiae Litterarum Caesareae Vindobonensis, Vindobonae, 1866–

*Declarationes in Sacram Regulam et Constitutiones Congregationis Helveto-Americanae O. S. B.,* St. Meinrad, Indiana: The Abbey Press, 1925.

*Decreta Authentica Congregationis Sacrorum Rituum,* 6 vols., Romae: Typis Polyglottis Vaticanis, 1898–1927.

Guignard, Philippe, *Les monuments primitifs de la Règle cistercienne publiés d'après les manuscrits de l'Abbaye de Cîteaux,* Analecta Divionensia, X, Dijon, 1878.

Jaffé, Philippus, *Regesta Pontificum Romanorum ab condita ecclesia ad annum post Christum natum MCXCVIII,* 2. ed. cura G. Wattenbach, S. Loewenfeld, F. Kaltenbrunner, P. Ewald, 2 vols. in 1, Lipsiae, 1885–1888.

Mansi, Ioannes, *Sacrorum Conciliorum Nova et Amplissima Collectio,* 53 vols. in 60, Paris-Leipzig-Arnhem, 1901–1927.

*Monumenta Germaniae Historica,* 188 vols. incomplete, Hannoverae, 1826–*Scriptores,* V, X, XII, ed. Georgius Henricus Pertz, Hannoverae, 1844, 1852, 1856; XIV, ed. Societas aperiendis fontibus rerum Germanicarum medii aevi, Hannoverae, 1883.

———, *Legum Sectio* III, *Concilia,* II, 1, recensuit Albertus Werminghoff, Hannoverae et Lipsiae, 1906.

*Regula et Constitutiones Generales Fratrum Minorum,* Ad Claras Aquas (Quaracchi) prope Florentiam: Ex typographia collegii S. Bonaventurae, 1922.

## AUTHORS

*A Short Breviary for Religious and the Laity,* ed. by monks of St. John's Abbey, 2. ed., Collegeville, Minn.: The Liturgical Press, 1942.

[Bachofen], Charles Augustine, *A Commentary on the New Code of Canon Law,* 8 vols., Vol. III, 5. ed., St. Louis: Herder, 1938.

Berlière, Ursmer, *L'Ordre monastique dès Origines au XII. Siècle,* 4. ed., Maredsous: Lille-Desclée, 1927.

Blat, Albertus, *Commentarium Textus Codicis Iuris Canonici,* 5 vols. in 6, Vol. II, 2. ed., Romae, 1921.

Blosius, Ludovicus, *The Paradise of the Faithful Soul, Part I—A Rule of the Spiritual Life (Canon Vitae Spiritualis),* anonymous translation revised and edited by Bernard Delany, O.P., London: Burns, Oates and Washbourne, Ltd., 1926.

Bouix, Dominicus, *Tractatus de Jure Regularium,* 2 vols., Parisiis, 1857.

Boyd, Catherine, *A Cistercian Nunnery in Mediaeval Italy—The Story of Rifreddo in Saluzzo, 1220-1300,* Harvard Historical Monographs, XVIII, Cambridge, Mass.: Harvard University Press, 1943.

Butzbach, Joh., *Wanderbüchlein,* Leipzig, 1912.

Chasles, Raymond, *Étude sur l'Institut monastique des Frères convers et sur l'Oblature au moyen Age,* unpublished dissertation, École des Chartes, Paris, 1906.

Cistercian Monk, A, *A Concise History of the Cistercian Order,* London, 1852.

Coronata, Matthaeus Conte a, *Institutiones Iuris Canonici,* 5 vols., Vol. I, Taurini: Marietti, 1928.

Creusen, Joseph — Garesché, Edward — Ellis, Adam, *Religious Men and Women in the Code,* 4. ed., Milwaukee: Bruce, 1942.

Delatte, Paul — McCann, Justin, *Commentary on the Rule of St. Benedict,* London, 1921.

Deroux, M. P., *Les Origines de l'Oblature bénédictine,* Les Éditions de la Revue Mabillon, I, Vienne: Abbaye Saint-Martin de Ligugé, 1927.

Donatus, Hyacinthus, *Rerum Regularium Praxis Resolutoria,* 4 vols., Coloniae Agrippinae, 1675.

Duchaussois, Pierre—Dawson, Thomas, *Hidden Apostles—Our Lay Brother Missionaries,* Ghent, Belgium: Imprimerie Erasmus, s. a., 1937.

Ernest, Brother, *Our Brothers,* Indianapolis: Scott, Foresman and Co., 1931.

Fanfani, Ludovicus, *De Iure Religiosorum ad normam Codicis Iuris Canonici,* 2. ed., Taurini-Romae: Marietti, 1925.

Ferraris, Lucius, *Prompta Bibliotheca, Canonica, Iuridica, Moralis, Theologica, nec non Ascetica, Polemica, Rubricistica, Historica,* 8 vols., Romae, 1766.

Fischer, Max, *Studien zur Entstehung der Hirsauener Konstitutionen,* Tübingen, 1910.

Frey, Wolfgang, *The Act of Religious Profession,* The Catholic University of America Canon Law Studies, n. 63, Washington, D. C.: The Catholic University of America Press, 1931.

*Guidonis Papae I Decisiones,* ed. Gasparis Baronis, Genevae, 1643.

Heimbucher, Max, *Die Orden und Kongregationen der katholischen Kirche,* 3. ed., 2 vols., Paderborn: Schöningh, 1933–1934.

Herrgott, Marquard, *Vetus disciplina monastica seu collectio auctorum O.S.B., qui ante sexcentos fere annos per Italiam, Galliam atque Germaniam de monastica disciplina tractarunt,* Parisiis, 1726.

Hilpisch, Stephanus, *Geschichte des benediktinischen Mönchtums,* Freiburg im Breisgau: Herder, 1929.

Hoffmann, Eberhard, *Das Konverseninstitut des Cisterzienserordens in seinem Ursprung und seiner Organisation,* Freiburger historische Studien, I, Freiburg, 1905.

Hunter-Blair, Oswald, *The Rule of St. Benedict edited with an English Translation and Explanatory Notes,* 4. ed., Fort Augustus: Abbey Press, 1934.

Hurter, Friedrich, *Geschichte Papst Innocenz' III und seiner Zeitgenossen,* 4 vols., Hamburg, 1844.

Kerker, Lic. M., *Wilhelm der Selige,* Tübingen, 1863.

Knowles, David, *The Monastic Order in England,* Cambridge: University Press, 1941.

Kreidler, Ildephonse, *The Fostering of Religious Vocations for the Brotherhood,* University of Notre Dame, Department of Education, Typed thesis in Notre Dame University Library, South Bend, Indiana, 1933.

*Lessons of the Temporal Cycle and the Principal Feasts of the Sanctoral Cycle according to the Monastic Breviary, compiled and adapted for the Office of the Brothers of St. Meinrad's Abbey, The,* St. Meinrad, Indiana: The Abbey Press, 1941.

*Lexikon für Theologie und Kirche,* 2. ed., herausgegeben von Michael Buchberger, 10 vols., Freiburg im Breisgau: Herder, 1930–1938.

Lezana, Johannes, *Summa Quaestionum Regularium,* 5 vols., Venetiis, 1654.

Linneborn, Johannes, *Der Zustand der westfälischen Benediktinerklöster in den letzten 50 Jahren vor ihrem Anschluss an die Bursfelder Kongregation,* Münster, 1898.

Lortz, Joseph, *History of the Church,* Translated and adapted from the 4th

German ed. by Edwin G. Kaiser, C.PP.S., S.T.D., Milwaukee: Bruce, 1938.

Mabillon, Johannes, *Annales Ordinis Sancti Benedicti*, ed. 1. Italica, 5 vols., Lucae, 1739–1740.

———, *Praefationes et Dissertationes V*, Tridenti, 1724.

Martène, Edmundus, *De Antiquis Ecclesiae Ritibus*, ed. novissima, 4 vols., Antuaerpiae-Venetiis, 1763–1764.

———, *De Antiquis Monachorum Ritibus*, Antuaerpiae-Venetiis, 1764.

Martène, Edmundus—Durand, Ursinus, *Thesaurus Novus Anecdotorum*, 5 vols., Lutetiae Parisiorum, 1717.

Mayer, Heinrich, *Benediktinisches Ordensrecht in der Beuroner Kongregation*, 4 vols., Beuron: Kunstverlag, 1929–1936.

McCann, Justin, *St. Benedict*, New York; Sheed and Ward, 1937.

Migne, Jacques, *Patrologiae Cursus Completus, Series Latina*, 221 vols., Parisiis, 1844–1864.

Mittarelli, Johannes — Costadoni, Anselmus, *Annales Camaldulenses Ordinis Sancti Benedicti*, 9 vols., Venetiis, 1755–1772.

Molitor, Raphael, *Religiosi Iuris Capita Selecta*, Ratisbonae, 1909.

Mulhern, Philip, *The Early Dominican Laybrother*, Washington, D. C.: [Dominican College], 1944.

Oesterle, Gerardus, *Praelectiones Iuris Canonici* (MS instar), Romae: Collegio S. Anselmi, 1931.

O'Neill, Francis, *The Dismissal of Religious in Temporary Vows*, The Catholic University of America Canon Law Studies, n. 166, Washington, D. C.: The Catholic University of America Press, 1942.

Paris, Julianus—Séjalon, Hugo, *Nomasticon Cisterciense*, 2. ed., Solesmis, 1892.

Pejška, Josephus, *Ius Canonicum Religiosorum*, 3. ed., Friburgi Brisgoviae: Herder, 1927.

Prümmer, Dominicus, *Manuale Iuris Canonici*, 3. ed., Friburgi Brisgoviae, 1922.

*Report of the Benedictine Brother Instructors' Convention, 1942*, St. Meinrad, Indiana: The Abbey Press, 1943.

Ringholz, Odilo, *Geschichte des fürstlichen Benediktinerstiftes U. L. F. von Einsiedeln*, u. s. w., Vol. I, from the time of St. Meinrad to the year 1526, Einsiedeln, 1904.

———, *Wallfahrtsgeschichte unserer Lieben Frau von Einsiedeln*, Freiburg im Breisgau, 1896.

Schaefer, Timotheus, *De Religiosis ad normam Codicis Iuris Canonici*, 3. ed., Roma: Herder, 1940.

Schröder, Richard—Künssberg, E. v., *Lehrbuch der deutschen Rechtsgeschichte*, 7. ed., Berlin-Leipzig: Verlag Walter de Gruyter and Co., 1932.

Schroll, Alfred, *Benedictine Monasticism as Reflected in the Warnefrid-Hildemar Commentaries on the Rule*, Studies in History, Economics and Public Law Edited by the Faculty of Political Science of Columbia University, n. 478, New York: Columbia University Press, 1941.

Schuetz, John, *The Origin of the Teaching Brotherhoods,* A Dissertation Submitted to the Faculty of Philosophy of the Catholic University of America in Partial Fulfillment of the Requirements for the Degree of Doctor of Philosophy, Washington, D. C., 1918.

Suarez, Franciscus, *Tractatus de Religione Societatis Jesu,* ed. De Reverseaux, Bruxellis-Parisiis, 1857.

*Thesaurus Linguae Latinae,* editus auctoritate et consilio Academiarum Quinque Germanicarum, Berolinsis, Gottingensis, Lipsiensis, Monacensis, Vindobonensis, 6 vols., incomplete, Lipsiae, 1900–

Thomas Aquinas, St., *Summa Theologica,* 6 vols., Taurini: Marietti, 1938.

Vacandard, Elphège, *Vie de St. Bernard,* 2 vols., Paris, 1895.

Vermeersch, Arthurus — Creusen, Iosephus, *Epitome Iuris Canonici,* 3 vols., Mechliniae-Romae: H. Dessain, 1936–1940. Vol. I, 6. ed., 1937.

Wernz, Franciscus, *Ius Decretalium,* 2. ed., 6 vols. in 7, Romae-Prati, 1905–1914.

Wolter, Maurus, *Praecipua Ordinis monastici Elementa,* Brugis, 1880.

## PERIODICALS

*America,* New York, 1909–

*Archiv für katholisches Kirchenrecht,* Innsbruck, 1857–1861; Mainz, 1862–

*Benediktinische Monatschrift,* Beuron, 1919–

*Catholic Mind, The,* New York, 1903–

*Commentarium pro Religiosis,* Romae, 1920–; ab anno 1935: *Commentarium pro Religiosis et Missionariis.*

*Ecclesiastical Review, The* (originally *The American Ecclesiastical Review*), Philadelphia, 1889–1943; Washington, D. C., 1944–

*Homiletic and Pastoral Review, The,* New York, 1900–

*Jurist, The,* Washington, D. C., 1941–

*Periodica de Re Canonica et Morali utili praesertim Religiosis et Missionariis,* Brugis, Romae, 1905–; ab anno 1927: *Periodica de Re Canonica, Morali, Liturgica.*

*Studien und Mitteilungen zur Geschichte des benediktiner- Ordens und seiner Zweige,* Brünn-Würzburg-Wien-München, 1880–

*Sword, The,* Englewood, N. J.-Washington, D. C., 1937–

*Zeitschrift für Kirchengeschichte,* Gotha, 1877–

## ARTICLES

(Anonymous), "Annotationes,"—*CpR,* I (1920), 354–356.

Altaner, B., "Zur Geschichte der mittelalterlichen Orden," *ZKG,* XLIX (1930), 54–56.

Beijersbergen, H., "De transitu religiosi de una classe ad alteram eiusdem religiosi instituti,"—*Periodica,* XXVI (1937), 33–37, 148–154.

Champoux, T., "The Clerical and Lay State versus the Religious State,"—*The Jurist,* I (1941), 135–138.

Dolberg, L., "Cistercienser- Mönche und Conversen als Landwirte und Arbeiter,"—*StudMittOSB,* XIII (1892), 216–228, 360–367, 503–512.

Ellis, A., "De Transitu ad aliam eiusdem Religionis Classem,"—*Periodica,* XXV (1936), 102*–104*.

Frison, B., "Ex-Seminarian and Novice: A Clarification,"—*The Jurist,* VI (1946), 416–418.

Garesché, E., "What Should Priests Think of the Brother's Vocation?"—*ER,* LXXIX (1928), 269–285.

———, "The Brothers Carry On but Need Young Recruits,"—*America,* LXVI (Nov. 29, 1941), 204–205.

———, "Congenial Soil for Vocations,"—*America,* LXVI (Feb. 14, 1942), 511–512.

———, "Influences in our Schools Unfavorable to Religious Vocations,"—*The Catholic Mind,* XL (June 22, 1942), 1–6.

Goyeneche, S., "Consultationes,"—*CpR,* III (1922), 10–13; 82–84; *CpRM,* XVII (1936), 79–81; XIX (1938), 13–14.

Larraona, A., "Commentarium,"—*CpR,* I (1920), 16–21; 46.

Ohligslager, M., "A New Approach in the Field of Vocations,"—*ER,* CIV (1941), 356–358.

Schaefers, W., "The Brother Problem,"—*The Homiletic and Pastoral Review,* XXXII (1931–1932), 61–67, 381–386.

———, "A Preparatory School for Brothers,"—*ER,* CIII (1940), 67–72.

Smet, J., "The Origin of the Carmelite Laybrothers,"—*The Sword,* VI (1942), 121–137.

Uhlhorn, G., "Der Einfluss der wirtschaftlichen Verhältnisse auf die Entwickelung des Mönchtums im Mittelalter,"—*ZKG,* XIV (1894), 347–403.

## ABBREVIATIONS

*AAS*—*Acta Apostolicae Sedis.*
Art.—Article.
*ASS*—*Acta Sanctae Sedis.*
Can.—Canon.
*CpR*—*Commentarium pro Religiosis.*
*CpRM*—*Commentarium pro Religiosis et Missionariis.*
*ER*—*The Ecclesiastical Review.*
*Fontes*—*Codicis Iuris Canonici Fontes cura . . . Gasparri editi.*
*Ibid.*—(*Ibidem*) The preceding reference.
*Loc. cit.*—*Loco citato.*
Mansi—*Sacrorum Conciliorum Nova et Amplissima Collectio.*
*MGH*—*Monumenta Germaniae Historica.*
*MPL*—Migne, *Patrologia Latina.*
*Op. cit.*—*Opere citato.*
*Periodica*—*Periodica de Re Canonica, Morali,* etc.
S. C. Ep. et Reg.—Sacra Congregatio Episcoporum et Regularium.
*SS*—*Scriptores.*
*StudMittOSB*—*Studien und Mitteilungen zur Geschichte des benediktiner-Ordens und seiner Zweige.*
*ZKG*—*Zeitschrift für Kirchengeschichte.*

# ALPHABETICAL INDEX

## BIOGRAPHICAL NOTE

Thomas Gerard Brockhaus was born in Humphrey, Nebraska, on April 22, 1914. After completing his elementary and high school education in Church and secular public schools in Nebraska and Oregon, he entered Mt. Angel Seminary conducted by the Benedictine Fathers at Mt. Angel, Oregon. He joined the Benedictine abbey there in 1933, where he also pursued his philosophical and theological studies, receiving the degree of Bachelor of Arts in 1936. He was ordained to the priesthood on May 18, 1939. He registered in the Graduate School of Canon Law at the Catholic University of America in February, 1940, and completed work for the degree of Bachelor of Canon Law in February, 1941, receiving the degree at the commencement exercises that year. He completed his work for the Licentiate in Canon Law in February, 1942, and was granted that degree at the commencement exercises in May, 1942.

## CANON LAW STUDIES*

1. FRERIKS, REV. CELESTINE A., C.PP.S., J.C.D., Religious Congregations in Their External Relations, 121 pp., 1916.
2. GALLIHER, REV. DANIEL M., O.P., J.C.D., Canonical Elections, 117 pp., 1917.
3. BORKOWSKI, REV. AURELIUS L., O.F.M., J.C.D., De Confraternitatibus Ecclesiasticis, 136 pp., 1918.
4. CASTILLO, REV. CAYO, J.C.D., Disertacion Historico-Canonica sobre la Potestad del Cabildo en Sede Vacante o Impedida del Vicario Capitular, 99 pp., 1919 (1918).
5. KUBELBECK, REV. WILLIAM J., S.T.B., J.C.D., The Sacred Penitentiaria and Its Relation to Faculties of Ordinaries and Priests, 129 pp., 1918.
6. PETROVITS, REV. JOSEPH J. C., S.T.D., J.C.D., The New Church Law on Matrimony, X-461 pp., 1919.
7. HICKEY, REV. JOHN J., S.T.B., J.C.D., Irregularities and Simple Impediments in the New Code of Canon Law, 100 pp., 1920.
8. KLEKOTKA, REV. PETER J., S.T.B., J.C.D., Diocesan Consultors, 179 pp., 1920.
9. WANENMACHER, REV. FRANCIS, J.C.D., The Evidence in Ecclesiastical Procedure Affecting the Marriage Bond, 1920 (Printed 1935).
10. GOLDEN, REV. HENRY FRANCIS, J.C.D., Parochial Benefices in the New Code, IV-119 pp., 1921 (Printed 1925).
11. KOUDELKA, REV. CHARLES J., J.C.D., Pastors, Their Rights and Duties According to the New Code of Canon Law, 211 pp., 1921.
12. MELO, REV. ANTONIUS, O.F.M., J.C.D., De Exemptione Regularium, X-188 pp., 1921.
13. SCHAAF, REV. VALENTINE THEODORE, O.F.M., S.T.B., J.C.D., The Cloister, X-180 pp., 1921.
14. BURKE, REV. THOMAS JOSEPH, S.T.D., J.C.D., Competence in Ecclesiastical Tribunals, IV-117 pp., 1922.
15. LEECH, REV. GEORGE LEO, J.C.D., A Comparative Study of the Constitution "Apostolicae Sedis" and the "Codex Juris Canonici," 179 pp., 1922.
16. MOTRY, REV. HUBERT LOUIS, S.T.D., J.C.D., Diocesan Faculties According to the Code of Canon Law, II-167 pp., 1922.
17. MURPHY, REV. GEORGE LAWRENCE, J.C.D., Delinquencies and Penalties in the Administration and the Reception of the Sacraments, IV-121 pp., 1923.

* Below n. 100 only numbers 25 and 57 are still available. Beginning with n. 100 only the following numbers are unavailable: Nos. 100–118 inclusive, and also n. 122.

18. O'Reilly, Rev. John Anthony, S.T.B., J.C.D., Ecclesiastical Sepulture in the New Code of Canon Law, II-129 pp., 1923.

19. Michalicka, Rev. Wenceslas Cyrill, O.S.B., J.C.D., Judicial Procedure in Dismissal of Clerical Exempt Religious, 107 pp., 1923.

20. Dargin, Rev. Edward Vincent, S.T.B., J.C.D., Reserved Cases According to the Code of Canon Law, IV-103 pp., 1924.

21. Godfrey, Rev. John A., S.T.B., J.C.D., The Right of Patronage According to the Code of Canon Law, 153 pp., 1924.

22. Hagedorn, Rev. Francis Edward, J.C.D., General Legislation on Indulgences, II-154 pp., 1924.

23. King, Rev. James Ignatius, J.C.D., The Administration of the Sacraments to Dying Non-Catholics, V-141 pp., 1924.

24. Winslow, Rev. Francis Joseph, O.F.M., J.C.D., Vicars and Prefects Apostolic, IV-149 pp., 1924.

25. Correa, Rev. Jose Servelion, S.T.L., J.C.D., La Potestad Legislativa de la Iglesia Catolica, IV-127 pp., 1925.

26. Dugan, Rev. Henry Francis, A.M., J.C.D., The Judiciary Department of the Diocesan Curia, 87 pp., 1925.

27. Keller, Rev. Charles Frederick, S.T.B., J.C.D., Mass Stipends, 167 pp., 1925.

28. Paschang, Rev. John Linus, J.C.D., The Sacramentals According to the Code of Canon Law, 129 pp., 1925.

29. Piontek, Rev. Cyrillus, O.F.M., S.T.B., J.C.D., De Indulto Exclaustrationis necnon Saecularizationis, XIII-289 pp., 1925.

30. Kearney, Rev. Richard Joseph, S.T.B., J.C.D., Sponsors at Baptism According to the Code of Canon Law, IV-127 pp., 1925.

31. Bartlett, Rev. Chester Joseph, A.M., LL.B., J.C.D., The Tenure of Parochial Property in the United States of America, V-108 pp., 1926.

32. Kilker, Rev. Adrian Jerome, J.C.D., Extreme Unction, V-425 pp., 1926.

33. McCormick, Rev. Robert Emmett, J.C.D., Confessors of Religious, VIII-266 pp., 1926.

34. Miller, Rev. Newton Thomas, J.C.D., Founded Masses According to the Code of Canon Law, VII-93 pp., 1926.

35. Roelker, Rev. Edward G., S.T.D., J.C.D., Principles of Privilege According to the Code of Canon Law, XI-166 pp., 1926.

36. Bakalarczyk, Rev. Richardus, M.I.C., J.U.D., De Novitiatu, VIII-208 pp., 1927.

37. Pizzuti, Rev. Lawrence, O.F.M., J.U.L., De Parochis Religiosis, 1927. (Not Printed.)

38. Bliley, Rev. Nicholas Martin, O.S.B., J.C.D., Altars According to the Code of Canon Law, XIX-132 pp., 1927.

39. Brown, Mr. Brendan Francis, A.B., LL.M., J.U.D., The Canonical Juristic Personality with Special Reference to its Status in the United States of America, V-212 pp., 1927.

40. CAVANAUGH, REV. WILLIAM THOMAS, C.P., J.U.D., The Reservation of the Blessed Sacrament, VIII-101 pp., 1927.
41. DOHENY, REV. WILLIAM J., C.S.C., A.B., J.U.D., Church Property: Modes of Acquisition, X-118 pp., 1927.
42. FELDHAUS, REV. ALOYSIUS H., C.PP.S., J.C.D., Oratories, IX-141 pp., 1927.
43. KELLY, REV. JAMES PATRICK, A.B., J.C.D., The Jurisdiction of the Simple Confessor, X-208 pp., 1927.
44. NEUBERGER, REV. NICHOLAS J., J.C.D., Canon 6 or the Relation of the Codex Juris Canonici to the Preceding Legislation, V-95 pp., 1927.
45. O'KEEFE, REV. GERALD MICHAEL, J.C.D., Matrimonial Dispensations, Powers of Bishops, Priests, and Confessors, VIII-232 pp., 1927.
46. QUIGLEY, REV. JOSEPH A. M., A.B., J.C.D., Condemned Societies, 139 pp., 1927.
47. ZAPLOTNIK, REV. JOHANNES LEO, J.C.D., De Vicariis Foraneis, X-142 pp., 1927.
48. DUSKIE, REV. JOHN ALOYSIUS, A.B., J.C.D., The Canonical Status of the Orientals in the United States, VIII-196 pp., 1928.
49. HYLAND, REV. FRANCIS EDWARD, J.C.D., Excommunication, Its Nature, Historical Development and Effects, VIII-181 pp., 1928.
50. REINMANN, REV. GERALD JOSEPH, O.M.C., J.C.D., The Third Order Secular of Saint Francis, 201 pp., 1928.
51. SCHENK, REV. FRANCIS J., J.C.D., The Matrimonial Impediments of Mixed Religion and Disparity of Cult, XVI-318 pp., 1929.
52. COADY, REV. JOHN JOSEPH, S.T.D., J.U.D., A.M., The Appointment of Pastors, VIII-150 pp., 1929.
53. KAY, REV. THOMAS HENRY, J.C.D., Competence in Matrimonial Procedure, VIII-164 pp., 1929.
54. TURNER, REV. SIDNEY JOSEPH, C.P., J.U.D., The Vow of Poverty, XLIX-217 pp., 1929.
55. KEARNEY, REV. RAYMOND A., A.B., S.T.D., J.C.D., The Principles of Delegation, VII-149 pp., 1929.
56. CONRAN, REV. EDWARD JAMES, A.B., J.C.D., The Interdict, V-163 pp., 1930.
57. O'NEILL, REV. WILLIAM H., J.C.D., Papal Rescripts of Favor, VII-218 pp., 1930.
58. BASTNAGEL, REV. CLEMENT VINCENT, J.U.D., The Appointment of Parochial Adjutants and Assistants, XV-257 pp., 1930.
59. FERRY, REV. WILLIAM A., A.B., J.C.D., Stole Fees, V-136 pp., 1930.
60. COSTELLO, REV. JOHN MICHAEL, A.B., J.C.D., Domicile and Quasi-Domicile, VII-201 pp., 1930.
61. KREMER, REV. MICHAEL NICHOLAS, A.B., S.T.B., J.C.D., Church Support in the United States, VI-136 pp., 1930.
62. ANGULO, REV. LUIS, C.M., J.C.D., Legislation de la Iglesia sobre la intencion en la application de la Santa Misa, VII-104 pp., 1931.

63. Frey, Rev. Wolfgang Norbert, O.S.B., A.B., J.C.D., The Act of Religious Profession, VIII-174 pp., 1931.
64. Roberts, Rev. James Brendan, A.B., J.C.D., The Banns of Marriage, XIV-140 pp., 1931.
65. Ryder, Rev. Raymond Aloysius, A.B., J.C.D., Simony, IX-151 pp., 1931.
66. Campagna, Rev. Angelo, Ph.D., J.U.D., Il Vicario Generale del Vescovo, VII-205 pp., 1931.
67. Cox, Rev. Joseph Godfrey, A.B., J.C.D., The Administration of Seminaries, VI-124 pp., 1931.
68. Gregory, Rev. Donald J., J.U.D., The Pauline Privilege, XV-165 pp., 1931.
69. Donohue, Rev. John F., J.C.D., The Impediment of Crime, VII-110 pp., 1931.
70. Dooley, Rev. Eugene A., O.M.I., J.C.D., Church Law on Sacred Relics, IX-143 pp., 1931.
71. Orth, Rev. Clement Raymond, O.M.C., J.C.D., The Approbation of Religious Institutes, 171 pp., 1931.
72. Pernicone, Rev. Joseph M., A.B., J.C.D., The Ecclesiastical Prohibition of Books, XII-267 pp., 1932.
73. Clinton, Rev. Connell, A.B., J.C.D., The Paschal Precept, IX-108 pp., 1932.
74. Donnelly, Rev. Francis B., A.M., S.T.L., J.C.D., The Diocesan Synod, VIII-125 pp., 1932.
75. Torrente, Rev. Camilo, C.M.F., J.C.D., Las Procesiones Sagradas, V-145 pp., 1932.
76. Murphy, Rev. Edwin J., C.PP.S., J.C.D., Suspension Ex Informata Conscientia, XI-122 pp., 1932.
77. MacKenzie, Rev. Eric F., A.M., S.T.L., J.C.D., The Delict of Heresy in its Commission, Penalization, Absolution, VII-124 pp., 1932.
78. Lyons, Rev. Avitus E., S.T.B., J.C.D., The Collegiate Tribunal of First Instance, XI-147 pp., 1932.
79. Connolly, Rev. Thomas A., J.C.D., Appeals, XI-195 pp., 1932.
80. Sangmeister, Rev. Joseph V., A.B., J.C.D., Force and Fear as Precluding Matrimonial Consent, V-211 pp., 1932.
81. Jaeger, Rev. Leo A., A.B., J.C.D., The Administration of Vacant and Quasi-Vacant Episcopal Sees in the United States, IX-229 pp., 1932.
82. Rimlinger, Rev. Herbert T., J.C.D., Error Invalidating Matrimonial Consent, VII-79 pp., 1932.
83. Barrett, Rev. John D. M., S.S., J.C.D., A Comparative Study of the Third Plenary Council of Baltimore and the Code, IX-221 pp., 1932.
84. Carberry, Rev. John J., Ph.D., S.T.D., J.C.D., The Juridical Form of Marriage, X-177 pp., 1934.
85. Dolan, Rev. John L., A.B., J.C.D., The Defensor Vinculi, XII-157 pp., 1934.

86. HANNAN, REV. JEROME D., A.M., S.T.D., LL.B., J.C.D., The Canon Law of Wills, IX-517 pp., 1934.
87. LEMIEUX, REV. DELISE A., A.M., J.C.D., The Sentence in Ecclesiastical Procedure, IX-131 pp., 1934.
88. O'ROURKE, REV. JAMES J., A.B., J.C.D., Parish Registers, VII-109 pp., 1934.
89. TIMLIN, REV. BARTHOLOMEW, O.F.M., A.M., J.C.D., Conditional Matrimonial Consent, X-381 pp., 1934.
90. WAHL, REV. FRANCIS X., A.B., J.C.D., The Matrimonial Impediments of Consanguinity and Affinity, VI-125 pp., 1934.
91. WHITE, REV. ROBERT J., A.B., LL.B., S.T.B., J.C.D., Canonical Ante-Nuptial Promises and the Civil Law, VI-152 pp., 1934.
92. HERRERA, REV. ANTONIO PARRA, O.C.D., J.C.D., Legislacion Ecclesiastica sobra el Ayuno y la Abstinencia, XI-191 pp., 1935.
93. KENNEDY, REV. EDWIN J., J.C.D., The Special Matrimonial Process in Cases of Evident Nullity, X-165 pp., 1935.
94. MANNING, REV. JOHN J., A.B., J.C.D., Presumption of Law in Matrimonial Procedure, XI-111 pp., 1935.
95. MOEDER, REV. JOHN M., J.C.D., The Proper Bishop for Ordination and Dimissorial Letters, VII-135 pp., 1935.
96. O'MARA, REV. WILLIAM A., A.B., J.C.D., Canonical Causes for Matrimonial Dispensations, IX-155 pp., 1935.
97. REILLY, REV. PETER, J.C.D., Residence of Pastors, IX-81 pp., 1935.
98. SMITH, REV. MARINER T., O.P., S.T.Lr., J.C.D., The Penal Law for Religious, VII-169 pp., 1935.
99. WHALEN, REV. DONALD W., A.M., J.C.D., The Value of Testimonial Evidence in Matrimonial Procedure, XIII-297 pp., 1935.
100. CLEARY, REV. JOSEPH F., J.C.D., Canonical Limitations on the Alienation of Church Property, VIII-141 pp., 1936.
101. GLYNN, REV. JOHN C., J.C.D., The Promoter of Justice, XX-337 pp., 1936.
102. BRENNAN, REV. JAMES H., S.S., M.A., S.T.B., J.C.D., The Simple Convalidation of Marriage, VI-135 pp., 1937.
103. BRUNINI, REV. JOSEPH BERNARD, J.C.D., The Clerical Obligations of Canons 139 and 142, X-121 pp., 1937.
104. CONNOR, REV. MAURICE, A.B., J.C.D., The Administrative Removal of Pastors, VIII-159 pp., 1937.
105. GUILFOYLE, REV. MERLIN JOSEPH, J.C.D., Custom, XI-144 pp., 1937.
106. HUGHES, REV. JAMES AUSTIN, A.B., A.M., J.C.D., Witnesses in Criminal Trials of Clerics, IX-140 pp., 1937.
107. JANSEN, REV. RAYMOND J., A.B., S.T.L., J.C.D., Canonical Provisions for Catechetical Instruction, VII-153 pp., 1937.
108. KEALY, REV. JOHN JAMES, A.B., J.C.D., The Introductory Libellus in Church Court Procedure, XI-121 pp., 1937.

109. McManus, Rev. James Edward, C.SS.R., J.C.D., The Administration of Temporal Goods in Religious Institutes, XVI-196 pp., 1937.
110. Moriarty, Rev. Eugene James, J.C.D., Oaths in Ecclesiastical Courts, X-115 pp., 1937.
111. Rainer, Rev. Eligius George, C.SS.R., J.C.D., Suspension of Clerics, XVII-249 pp., 1937.
112. Reilly, Rev. Thomas F., C.SS.R., J.C.D., Visitation of Religious, VI-195 pp., 1938.
113. Moriarty, Rev. Francis E. C.SS.R., J.C.D., The Extraordinary Absolution from Censures, XV-334 pp., 1938.
114. Connolly, Rev. Nicholas P., J.C.D., The Canonical Erection of Parishes, X-132 pp., 1938.
115. Donovan, Rev. James Joseph, J.C.D., The Pastor's Obligation in Prenuptial Investigation, XII-322 pp., 1938.
116. Harrigan, Rev. Robert J., M.A., S.T.B., J.C.D., The Radical Sanation of Invalid Marriages, VIII-208 pp., 1938.
117. Boffa, Rev. Conrad Humbert, J.C.D., Canonical Provisions for Catholic Schools, VII-211 pp., 1939.
118. Parsons, Rev. Anscar John, O.M.Cap., J.C.D., Canonical Elections, XII-236 pp., 1939.
119. Reilly, Rev. Edward Michael, A.B., J.C.D., The General Norms of Dispensation, XII-156 pp., 1939.
120. Ryan, Rev. Gerald Aloysius, A.B., J.C.D., Principles of Episcopal Jurisdiction, XII-172 pp., 1939.
121. Burton, Rev. Francis James, C.S.C., A.B., J.C.D., A Commentary on Canon 1125, X-222 pp., 1940.
122. Miaskiewicz, Rev. Francis Sigismund, J.C.D., Supplied Jurisdiction According to Canon 209, XII-340 pp., 1940.
123. Rice, Rev. Patrick William, A.B., J.C.D., Proof of Death in Prenuptial Investigation, VIII-156 pp., 1940.
124. Anglin, Rev. Thomas Francis, M.S., J.C.D., The Eucharistic Fast, VIII-183 pp., 1941.
125. Coleman, Rev. John Jerome, J.C.D., The Minister of Confirmation, VI-153 pp., 1941.
126. Downs, Rev. Joseph Emmanuel, A.B., J.C.D., The Concept of Clerical Immunity, XI-163 pp., 1941.
127. Esswein, Rev. Anthony Albert, J.C.D., Extrajudicial Penal Powers of Ecclesiastical Superiors, X-144 pp., 1941.
128. Farrell, Rev. Benjamin Francis, M.A., S.T.L., J.C.D., The Rights and Duties of the Local Ordinary Regarding Congregations of Women Religious of Pontifical Approval, V-195 pp., 1941.
129. Feeney, Rev. Thomas John, A.B., S.T.L., J.C.D., Restitutio in Integrum, VI-169 pp., 1941.
130. Findlay, Rev. Stephen William, O.S.B., A.B., J.C.D., Canonical

Norms Governing the Deposition and Degradation of Clerics, XVII-279 pp., 1941.

131. Goodwine, Rev. John, A.B., S.T.L., J.C.D., The Right of the Church to Acquire Property, VIII-119 pp., 1941.

132. Heston, Rev. Edward Louis, C.S.C., Ph.D., S.T.D., J.C.D., The Alienation of Church Property in the United States, XII-222 pp., 1941.

133. Hogan, Rev. James John, A.B., S.T.L., J.C.D., Judicial Advocates and Procurators, XIII-200 pp., 1941.

134. Kealy, Rev. Thomas M., A.B., Litt.B., J.C.D., Dowry of Women Religious, IX-152 pp., 1941.

135. Keene, Rev. Michael James, O.S.B., J.C.D., Religious Ordinaries and Canon 198, V-164 pp., 1942.

136. Kerin, Rev. Charles A., S.S., M.A., S.T.B., J.C.D., The Privation of Christian Burial, XVI-279 pp., 1941.

137. Louis, Rev. William Francis, M.A., J.C.D., Diocesan Archives, X-101 pp., 1941.

138. McDevitt, Rev. Gilbert Joseph, A.B., J.C.D., Legitimacy and Legitimation, X-247 pp., 1941.

139. McDonough, Rev. Thomas Joseph, A.B., J.C.D., Apostolic Administrators, X-217 pp., 1941.

140. Meier, Rev. Carl Anthony, A.B., J.C.D., Penal Administrative Procedure Against Negligent Pastors, XI-240 pp., 1941.

141. Schmidt, Rev. John Rogg, A.B., J.C.D., The Principles of Authentic Interpretation in Canon 17 of the Code of Canon Law, XII-331 pp., 1941.

142. Slafkosky, Rev. Andrew Leonard, A.B., J.C.D., The Canonical Episcopal Visitation of the Diocese, X-197 pp., 1941.

143. Swoboda, Rev. Innocent Robert, O.F.M., J.C.D., Ignorance in Relation to the Imputability of Delicts, IX-271 pp., 1941.

144. Dubé, Rev. Arthur Joseph, A.B., J.C.D., The General Principles for the Reckoning of Time in Canon Law, VIII-299 pp., 1941.

145. McBride, Rev. James T., A.B., J.C.D., Incardination and Excardination of Seculars, XX-585 pp., 1941.

146. Król, Rev. John T., J.C.D., The Defendant in Contentious Trials, XII-207 pp., 1942.

147. Comyns, Rev. Joseph J., C.SS.R., A.B., J.C.D., Papal and Episcopal Administration of Church Property, XIV-155 pp., 1942.

148. Barry, Rev. Garrett Francis, O.M.I., J.C.D., Violation of the Cloister, XII-260 pp., 1942.

149. Bolduc, Rev. Gatien, C.S.V., A.B., S.T.L., J.C.D., Les Études dans les Religions Cléricales, VIII-155 pp., 1942.

150. Boyle, Rev. David John, M.A., J.C.D., The Juridic Effects of Moral Certitude on Pre-Nuptial Guarantees, XII-188 pp., 1942.

151. Canavan, Rev. Walter Joseph, M.A., Litt.D., J.C.D., The Profession of Faith, XII-143 pp., 1942.

152. **DESROCHERS, REV. BRUNO, A.B., Ph.L., S.T.B., J.C.D., Le Premier** Concile Plénier de Québec et le Code de Droit Canonique, XIV-186 pp., 1942.
153. DILLON, REV. ROBERT EDWARD, A.B., J.C.D., Common Law Marriage, X-148 pp., 1942.
154. **DODWELL, REV. EDWARD JOHN, Ph.D., S.T.B., J.C.D., The Time and** Place for the Celebration of Marriage, X-156 pp., 1942.
155. DONNELLAN, REV. THOMAS ANDREW, A.B., J.C.D., The Obligation of the Missa pro Populo, VII-131 pp., 1942.
156. ELTZ, REV. LOUIS ANTHONY, A.B., J.C.D., Cooperation in Crime, XII-208 pp., 1942.
157. GASS, REV. SYLVESTER FRANCIS, M.A., J.C.D., Ecclesiastical Pensions, XI-206 pp., 1942.
158. GUINIVEN, REV. JOHN JOSEPH, C.SS.R., J.C.D., The Precept of Hearing Mass, XIV-188 pp., 1942.
159. GULCZYNSKI, REV. JOHN THEOPHILUS, J.C.D., The Desecration and Violation of Churches, X-126 pp., 1942.
160. HAMMILL, REV. JOHN LEO, M.A., J.C.D., The Obligations of the Traveler According to Canon 14, VIII-204 pp., 1942.
161. HAYDT, REV. JOHN JOSEPH, A.B., J.C.D., Reserved Benefices, XI-148 pp., 1942.
162. HUSER, REV. ROGER JOHN, O.F.M., A.B., J.C.D., The Crime of Abortion in Canon Law, XII-187 pp., 1942.
163. **KEARNEY, REV. FRANCIS PATRICK, A.B., S.T.L., J.C.D., The Principles of Canon 1127, X-162 pp., 1942.**
164. LINAHEN, REV. LEO JAMES, S.T.L., J.C.D., De Absolutione Complicis In Peccato Turpi, 114 pp., 1942.
165. MCCLOSKEY, REV. JOSEPH ALOYSIUS, A.B., J.C.D., The Subject of Ecclesiastical Law According to Canon 12, XVII-246 pp., 1942.
166. O'NEILL, REV. FRANCIS JOSEPH, C.SS.R., J.C.D., The Dismissal of Religious in Temporary Vows, XIII-220 pp., 1942.
167. **PRINCE, REV. JOHN EDWARD, A.B., S.T.B., J.C.D., The Diocesan Chan**cellor, X-136 pp., 1942.
168. RIESNER, REV. ALBERT JOSEPH, C.SS.R., J.C.D., Apostates and Fugitives from Religious Institutes, IX-168 pp., 1942.
169. STENGER, REV. JOSEPH BERNARD, J.C.D., The Mortgaging of Church Property, 186 pp., 1942.
170. WALDRON, REV. JOSEPH FRANCIS, A.B., J.C.D., The Minister of Baptism, XII-197 pp., 1942.
171. WILLETT, REV. ROBERT ALBERT, J.C.D., The Probative Value of Documents in Ecclesiastical Trials, X-124 pp., 1942.
172. WOEBER, REV. EDWARD MARTIN, M.A., J.C.D., The Interpellations, XII-161 pp., 1942.
173. BENKO, REV. MATTHEW ALOYSIUS, O.S.B., M.A., J.C.D., The Abbot *Nullius*, XIV-148 pp., 1943.

174. Christ, Rev. Joseph James, M.A., S.T.L., J.C.D., Dispensation from Vindicative Penalties, XIV-285 pp., 1943.
175. Clancy, Rev. Patrick M. J., O.P., A.B., S.T.Lr., J.C.D., The Local Religious Superior, X-229 pp., 1943.
176. Clarke, Rev. Thomas James, J.C.D., Parish Societies, XII-147 pp., 1943.
177. Connolly, Rev. John Patrick, S.T.L., J.C.D., Synodal Examiners and Parish Priest Consultors, X-223 pp., 1943.
178. Drumm, Rev. William Martin, A.B., J.C.D., Hospital Chaplains, XII-175 pp., 1943.
179. Flanagan, Rev. Bernard Joseph, A.B., S.T.L., J.C.D., The Canonical Erection of Religious Houses, X-147 pp., 1943.
180. Kelleher, Rev. Stephen Joseph, A.B., S.T.B., J.C.D., Discussions with Non-Catholics: Canonical Legislation, X-93 pp., 1943.
181. Lewis, Rev. Gordian, C.P., J.C.D., Chapters in Religious Institutes, XII-169 pp., 1943.
182. Marx, Rev. Adolph, J.C.D., The Declaration of Nullity of Marriages Contracted Outside the Church, X-151 pp., 1943.
183. Matulenas, Rev. Raymond Anthony, O.S.B., A.B., J.C.D., Communication, a Source of Privileges, XII-225 pp., 1943.
184. O'Leary, Rev. Charles Gerard, C.SS.R., J.C.D., Religious Dismissed After Perpetual Profession, X-213 pp., 1943.
185. Power, Rev. Cornelius Michael, J.C.D., The Blessing of Cemeteries, XII-231 pp., 1943.
186. Shuhler, Rev. Ralph Vincent, O.S.A., J.C.D., Privileges of Regulars to Absolve and Dispense, XII-195 pp., 1943.
187. Ziolkowski, Rev. Thaddeus Stanislaus, A.B., J.C.D., The Consecration and Blessing of Churches, XII-151 pp., 1943.
188. Heneghan, Rev. John Joseph, S.T.D., J.C.D., The Marriages of Unworthy Catholics: Canons 1065 and 1066, XVI-213 pp., 1944.
189. Carroll, Rev. Coleman Francis, M.A., S.T.L., J.C.L., Charitable Institutions.
190. Ciesluk, Rev. Joseph Edward, Ph.B., S.T.L., J.C.L., National Parishes in the United States.
191. Coburn, Rev. Vincent Paul, A.B., J.C.D., Marriages of Conscience, XII-172 pp., 1944.
192. Connors, Rev. Charles Paul, C.S.Sp., A.B., J.C.D., Extra-Judicial Procurators in the Code of Canon Law, X-94 pp., 1944.
193. Coyle, Rev. Paul Raymond, A.B., J.C.D., Judicial Exceptions, X-142 pp., 1944.
194. Fair, Rev. Bartholomew Francis, A.B., S.T.L., J.C.L., The Impediment of Abduction.
195. Gallagher, Rev. Thomas Raphael, O.P., A.B., S.T.Lr., J.C.D., The Examination of the Qualities of the Ordinand, X-166 pp., 1944.
196. Gannon, Rev. John Mark, S.T.L., J.C.D., The Interstices Required for the Promotion to Orders, XII-100 pp., 1944.

197. GOLDSMITH, REV. J. WILLIAM, B.C.S., S.T.L., J.C.D., The Competence of Church and State over Marriage—Disputed Points, X-128 pp., 1944.
198. GOODWINE, REV. JOSEPH GERARD, A.B., S.T.B., J.C.D., The Reception of Converts, XIV-326 pp., 1944.
199. KOWALSKI, REV. ROMUALD EUGENE, O.F.M., A.B., J.C.D., Sustenance of Religious Houses of Regulars, X-174 pp., 1944.
200. MCCOY, REV. ALAN EDWARD, O.F.M., J.C.D., Force and Fear in Relation to Delictual Imputability and Penal Responsibility, XII-160 pp., 1944.
201. MCDEVITT, REV. VINCENT JOHN, Ph.B., S.T.L., J.C.L., Perjury.
202. MARTIN, REV. THOMAS OWEN, Ph.D., S.T.D., J.C.D., Adverse Possession, Prescription and Limitation of Actions: The Canonical "Praescriptio," XX-208 pp., 1944.
203. MIKLOSOVIC, REV. PAUL JOHN, A.B., J.C.L., Attempted Marriages and Their Consequent Juridic Effects.
204. MUNDY, REV. THOMAS MAURICE, A.B., S.T.L., J.C.D., The Union of Parishes, X—164 pp., 1945.
205. O'DEA, REV. JOHN COYLE, A.B., J.C.D., The Matrimonial Impediment of Nonage, VIII-126 pp., 1944.
206. OLALIA, REV. ALEXANDER AYSON, S.T.L., J.C.D., A Comparative Study of the Christian Constitution of States and the Constitution of the Philippine Commonwealth, XII—136 pp., 1944.
207. POISSON, REV. PIERRE-MARIE, C.S.C., A.B., Ph.L., Th.L., J.C.L., Droits Patrimoniaux des Maisons et des Églises Religieuses.
208. STADALNIKAS, REV. CASIMIR JOSEPH, M.I.C., J.C.D., Reservation of Censures, X-141 pp., 1944.
209. SULLIVAN, REV. EUGENE HENRY, S.T.L., J.C.D., Proof of the Reception of the Sacraments, X—165 pp., 1944.
210. VAUGHAN, REV. WILLIAM EDWARD, J.C.D., Constitutions for Diocesan Courts, X-210 pp., 1944.
211. PARO, REV. GINO, S.T.D., J.C.L., The Right of Apostolic Legation.
212. BALZER, REV. RALPH FRANCIS, C.P., J.C.L., The Computation of Time in a Canonical Novitiate.
213. DOUGHERTY, REV. JOHN WHELAN, A.B., S.T.L., J.C.L., De Inquisitione Speciali.
214. DZIOB, REV. MICHAEL WALTER, J.C.L., The Sacred Congregation for the Oriental Church.
215. EIDENSCHINK, REV. JOHN ALBERT, O.S.B., B.A., J.C.L., The Election of Bishops in the Letters of Pope Gregory the Great.
216. GILL, REV. NICHOLAS, C.P., J.C.L., The Spiritual Prefect in Clerical Religious Houses of Study.
217. HYNES, REV. HARRY GERARD, S.T.L., J.C.D., The Privileges of Cardinals, XII-183 pp., 1945.
218. MCDEVITT, REV. GERALD VINCENT, S.T.L., J.C.D., The Renunciation of an Ecclesiastical Office, XIV—179 pp., 1946.

219. MANNING, REV. JOSEPH LEROY, J.C.L., The Free Conferral of Offices.
220. MEYER, REV. LOUIS G., O.S.B., A.B., S.T.B., J.C.D., Alms-Gathering by Religious, XII—163 pp., 1946.
221. O'DONNELL, REV. CLETUS FRANCIS, M.A., J.C.L., The Marriage of Minors.
222. PRUNSKIS, REV. JOSEPH, J.C.D., Comparative Law, Ecclesiastical and Civil, in Lithuanian Concordat, X—161 pp., 1945.
223. SWEENEY, REV. FRANCIS PATRICK, C.SS.R., J.C.D., The Reduction of Clerics to the Lay State, X—199 pp., 1945.
224. VOGELPOHL, REV. HENRY JOHN, J.C.L., The Simple Impediments to Holy Orders.
225. BROCKHAUS, REV. THOMAS AQUINAS, O.S.B., A.B., J.C.L., Religious who Are Known as *Conversi*.

www.ingramcontent.com/pod-product-compliance
Lightning Source LLC
LaVergne TN
LVHW050207080826
844660LV00012B/375

* 9 7 8 0 8 1 3 2 2 4 0 9 1 *